LAND OF GENGHIS KHAN

THE RISE AND FALL OF NATION-STATES IN CHINA'S NORTHERN FRONTIERS

DAVID CHUENYAN LAI

WESTERN GEOGRAPHICAL SERIES, VOLUME 30

editorial address

Harold D. Foster, Ph.D.
Department of Geography
University of Victoria
Victoria, British Columbia
Canada

Since publication began in 1970 the Western Geographical Series has been generously supported by the Leon and Thea Koerner Foundation, the Social Science Federation of Canada, the National Centre for Atmospheric Research, the International Geographical Union Congress, the University of Victoria, the Natural Sciences Engineering Research Council of Canada, the Institute of the North American West, the University of Regina, the Potash and Phosphate Institute of Canada, the Saskatchewan Agriculture and Food Department, and the B.C. Ministry of Health and Ministry Responsible for Seniors.

COPYRIGHT 1995, UNIVERSITY OF VICTORIA

LAND OF GENGHIS KHAN

(Western geographical series, ISSN 0315-2022; v. 30)
Includes bibliographical references.
ISBN 0-919838-20-0

1. Mongolia—History. 2 Mongolia—Civilization. I. University of Victoria (B.C.). Dept. of Geography. II. Title. III. Series.

DS798.5.L34 1995   951'.7   C95-910121-7

ACKNOWLEDGEMENTS

Several members of the Department of Geography, University of Victoria co-operated to ensure the successful publication of this volume of the Western Geographical Series. Special thanks are due to members of the technical services division. Diane Macdonald undertook the very demanding task of typesetting, while cartography was in the expert hands of Ole Heggen. Ken Josephson designed the cover and produced the excellent line drawings. Their dedication and hard work is greatly appreciated.

University of Victoria   Harold D. Foster
Univeria, British Columbia   Series Editor
January 9, 1995

Plate 1   *Genghis Khan (previous page)*

TABLE OF CONTENTS

List of Figures ii

List of Tables ii

List of Plates iii

Preface iv

1   Introduction 1

2   Land and People 8

3   The Donghu and Xiongnu in the Warring States Period, 475-221 B.C. 12

4   The Xiongnu Empire in the Han Dynasty, 206 B.C.- A.D. 220 15

5   The Five Nomadic Tribes in the Eastern Jin Dynasty, 217-420 19

6   The Tujue Empire in the Sui and Tang Dynasties, 581-907 22

7   The Emergence of a Qidan State in the Five Dynasties Period, 907-960 26

8   The Triumvirate of the Qidan, Dangxiang and Han People in the Northern Song Dynasty, 960-1127 29

9   The Emergence of the Jin and Xiliao States in the Southern Song Dynasty, 1127-1279 33

10 The Mongol Empire of Genghis Khan, 1227 35

11 The Establishment of the Yuan Dynasty by Khubilai Khan, 1271-1368 41

12 The Khalkhas and Oirats in the Ming Dynasty, 1368-1644 45

13 Inner and Outer Mongolia During the Qing Dynasty, 1644-1911 49

14 The Emergence of the Mongolian People's Republic, 1924-1946 52

15 The Establishment of Inner Mongolian Autonomous Region, 1947 55

16 Epilogue 62

References 64

Glossary (地名、人名、朝代、民族及其他之名稱) 69

The Author 76

List of Figures

1. Political Divisions of People's Republic of China, 1994 4
2. The Relief of the Inner Mongolian Autonomous Region 6
3. The Donghu and Xiongnu in the Period of the Warring States, 475-221 B.C. 13
4. The Xiongnu Empire in the Han Dynasty, 206 B.C.- A.D. 220 16
5. The Distribution of Nomadic Tribes in North China During the Eastern Jin Dynasty, 217-420 20
6. The Tujue Empire in the Tang Dynasty, 618-907 23
7. The Expansion of the Liao State in the Period of Five Dynasties, 907-960 27
8. The Location of the Liao and Xixia States in the Northern Song Dynasty, 960-1127 30
9. Plans of Nanjing, Zhongdu, Dadu, and Beijing 31
10. The Distribution of States formed by Nomadic Tribes in the Southern Song Dynasty, 1127-1279 34
11. The Extent of the Mongol Empire of Genghis Khan, 1227 36
12. The Yuan Empire of Khubilai Khan, 1271-1368 42
13. Location of the Khalkhas and Oirats in the Ming Dynasty, 1368-1644 46
14. Inner and Outer Mongolia in the Qing Dynasty, 1670 50
15. The Reorganization of Inner Mongolia, 1928 54
16. The Boundary of the Inner Mongolian Autonomous Region, 1953 57
17. The Boundary of the Inner Mongolian Autonomous Region, 1957-1968 59
18. The Boundary of the Inner Mongolian Autonomous Region, 1969-1978 60
19. Political Divisions of the Inner Mongolian Autonomous Region, 1994 61

List of Tables

1. Names of Nomadic Tribes in Different Chinese Dynasties 3
2. Name and Location of the Sixteen States, 304-443 21
3. The Five Dynasties and Ten Kingdoms, 907-960 28
4. The Ethnic Composition of China's Population, 1990 56
5. Distribution of Mongols in China, 1990 58
6. The Ethnic Composition of Inner Mongolia, 1990 58

List of Plates

1. Genghis Khan ....frontispiece

2. A Group of Mongolian Devotees in the Gandan Monastery, Ulaan Baatar v

3. Young Kazakh in Bayan Ulgi, Kazakh Mongolia vi

4. A Kirghiz Yurt 11

5. A Mongolian Lama of the Yellow Sect 14

6. The Ruined City of Jiaohe Near Turpan on the Silk Road,
    Once a Flourishing City During the Tang Dynasty (A.D. 618-907) 18

7. A Khalkha Girl 21

8. A Lama Monastery in a Village Near Hohhot 25

9. A Khalkha Rider on a Typical Mongolian Pony 28

10. "The Turtle," a Spectacular Geological Formation
    South of the Town of Dadal, Province of Khentiy, Mongolia 32

11. This Boulder Marks the Site of the Legendary Birthplace of Genghis Khan,
    Near the Town of Dadal, About 300 km Northeast of Ulaan Baatar 40

12. Khubilai Khan 44

13. A Khalkha Horseman 48

14. A Kazakh Woman Milking a Cow 51

15. Typical Mongolian Camels 64

CREDITS:

Dr. Ted Owen: Plates 4, 6, 8, 15

PREFACE

Archaeological excavations in the Inner Mongolian Autonomous Region of China during the past 45 years have discovered many priceless artifacts that shed light on the artistic work and technological development of the nomadic tribes such as the Donghu, Xiongnu, Xianbei, Qidan (Khitan), and Dangxiang in the northern frontiers of China. Who are these nomadic people bearing such unfamiliar names? Where were little known states such as Xixia, Xiliao and Huigu? What are these names in Chinese characters? What was the power relationship between these non-Han nomads and the Han agriculturalists in each Chinese dynasty? In addition to answering these questions, this book is aimed at students, teachers and the general public who are interested in the history of the Eurasian nomads of China's northern frontiers.

There are many variations in the romanization and transliteration of Chinese names. For the sake of consistency, the Pinyin system of romanization has been used in this book wherever possible. The following is a table of some Chinese Phonetic Alphabets showing pronunciation with approximate English equivalents. The Wade-Giles spelling or customary English transcription are given in brackets.

(A) Initials

d	(t)	as in **d**o, **d**ay[1]
g	(k)	as in s**k**ill, **g**ay[1]
j	(ch)	as in **j**eep[2]
q	(ch)	as in **ch**eek, **ch**eer[2]
x	(hs)	as "sh" in **sh**e[2]
zh	(ts)	as "j" in **j**ump, **j**u**dge**[1 and 3]

[1] vocal cords do not vibrate.

[2] Tip of tongue touches the hard palate.

[3] Tip of tongue is slightly curled.

(B) Finals

e	as in h**er**
ei	as in **ei**ght
eng	as s**ung**
iang	as **young** (approximately)
iao	as **yow**l
ia	as **A**s**ia**
ie	as **ye**s
iong	**i + ong**
o	as in s**aw**
ong	as **ung** (German)
ua	as **wa**ft (**u + a**)
uai	as **wi**fe (**u + ai**)
uan	as **wan**der (**u + an**), **one** (approximately)
uang	as **wang** (**u + ang**)
ui	as **we** or **way** (**u + ei**)
un	as **wen**t (approximately)
uo	as **wo**man, **wa**ll

I am grateful to Professor Jiang Changyu of East China Normal University for providing me with information about the changing boundaries of the Inner Mongolian Autonomous Region, and Mr. Mark Yaolin Wang of the University of British Columbia for sending 1990 Census data on ethnic groups in China and Inner Mongolia. Thanks also to Dr. Elizabeth Kennedy, Messrs Ron Lou-Poy, Jack Lee, Phil Thornton-Joe; Ms May Lou-Poy, Charlayne Thornton-Joe, Roberta Lai; and an anonymous reviewer for proof-reading drafts and giving valuable suggestions for their improvement. I am in debt to Dr. Harold Foster for editing the manuscript. Thanks are given to Mr. Sam Lum for writing the book title in Chinese characters.

Plate 2   *A Group of Mongolian Devotees in the Gandan Monastery, Ulaan Baatar (above)*

Plate 3   *Young Kazakh in Bayan Ulgi, Kazakh Mongolia (following page)*

INTRODUCTION

The early history of China's northern frontiers is a litany of war and peace between the agriculturalists of the Chinese or Han people in the Huang He (Yellow River) basin, and the non-Han pastoral tribes who roamed across the Mongolian deserts and grassland. (Hereafter, the Chinese are referred to as the Han people). For thousands of years the Han farmers and the Non-Han nomads fought over the more fertile and productive land in China's northern frontiers. When the pastoralists were united and strong, they would invade the Han people. When they were disunited, the Han people would subjugate them. However, military alliances and cultural interaction are also a significant feature in the history of China's northern frontiers. These Han and Non-Han alliances have broken down the dichotomy of the northern nomads and southern agriculturalists in Chinese history.

In the historical past, small groups of Mongolian tribes lived together and pastured their herds on grassland. Each tribe was led by a chieftain (known as a khan or chanyu) who rose to power through personal bravery and prowess. Occasionally a strong and able leader might succeed in uniting several nomadic tribes as a confederation. However, such confederations did not form a true state, kingdom, or empire since their grassland did not have boundaries defined by geography, or history, nor did they have a system of towns and cities. After a confederation was broken up by intra-tribal wars, or by external powers, the nomadic tribes would be scattered until another strong leader emerged to reunite them. This cyclic pattern of disunion-confederation-disunion was repeated throughout the Mongol history. The Mongolian nomads assimilated and inter-married with members of rival tribes after they vanquished them. When they themselves were conquered, they would be assimilated by their opponents. Hence, it is difficult to trace the ethnic origins of the Mongolian nomads.

The Eurasian nomads in China's northern frontiers can be classified into three major linguistic groups, namely the Tungusic-speaking (the Huns), Turkic-speaking (the Turks), and Mongolian-speaking people, but their tribal subdivisions are often obscure and confusing. Some linguists consider the Mongolian-speaking people as one of the Tungusic-speaking subgroups. Of all the Eurasian nomadic tribes, the

Mongolians are by far the best known mainly because Genghis Khan (c.1162-1227) established an extensive Mongol Empire from the Pacific coast across Asia to Eastern Europe. The Mongolians are not a single nomadic tribe and comprise many affiliate groups. There are five hypotheses concerning their origin (Xue Xin, 1944, pp.5-6). The first is that the Mongolians were descendants of the Donghu, who consisted of many sub-groups such as the Shiwei, Xianbei, and Wuhuan (Table 1). These sub-groups were further divided into many clans. Complicating the issue further, some tribes changed their names after they established states. The Kiyat clan, for example, became more popularly known as the Mongols after their leader, Genghis Khan, established the Mongol Empire. A second hypothesis is that the Mongolians were descendants of the Xiongnu whose homeland was on the Mongolian Plateau. Different branches of the Xiongnu are thought also to have migrated to eastern Europe, later to become the Huns, ancestors of the Hungarians. A third hypothesis is that the Mongolians were descendants of the Tujue. As early as the eighth century A.D. they called themselves the Menggu (Mongol) and were known to the Han people as the Mengwu, Shiwei or Mengwu Shiwei. Later they were called the Black Tatars by the Manchu who established the Qing Dynasty in China. According to a fourth hypothesis, the Mongolians were descendants of the Tufan (Tibetans).

However, many historians believe that the Mongolians were, in fact, descendants of mixed Donghu and Tujue, mixed Shiwei and Xiongnu, or mixed Donghu, Xiongnu, and Tujue (Sun, 1951, p.28). The Mongols consider themselves to be descendants of the nomadic tribes living in the Taiga (sub-arctic coniferous forest) near Lake Baikal. Clearly there is no agreement, and the origin of the Mongolians is still disputable. To further complicate the situation, the Mongolians were called different names in various Chinese dynasties by the Han people. They were known, for example, as the Di, Quan Rong, and Donghu during the Eastern Zhou Dynasty (770-256 B.C.), but their descendants were later called the Xiongnu, Xianbei, Qidan (Khitan), Moge, or Nuzhen. In Chinese historic records, different groups of Turkic-speaking pastoralists on the Mongolian Plateau had distinct names, such as the Ruanruan (Rouran), Tujue, Huiqi (Uygurs), or Kirghiz. From time to time, these nomadic tribes formed and broke alliances, and assimilated other natives and were themselves assimilated. It is very difficult, therefore, to differentiate between ethnic groups in China's northern frontiers.

The Mongolian Plateau is a single physical region, however in the seventeenth century, it was divided politically by the Manchu. They coined the names "Outer Mongolia" for the land north of the Gobi Desert and "Inner Mongolia" for the land south

Table 1 Names of Nomadic Tribes in Different Chinese Dynasties

Dynasty	Period	Tungusic-speaking	Turkic-speaking	Tibetan-speaking
E. Zhou	770 - 256 B.C.	Hu < Di / Quan Rong		Qiang
Qin	221 - 207 B.C.	Hu < Donghu / Xiongnu		
Han	206 B.C. - A.D. 220	Donghu < Shiwei / Xianbei / Wuhuan		Xiqiang
Jin N. & S. Dynasties Sui	265-420 420-589 581-618	Xianbei < Tuoba Xianbei / Other Xianbei tribes	Ruanruan	Qiang
Tang Five Dynasties	618-907 907-960	Menggu (Mongols) < Mengwu Shiwei / Tatars Moge < Heishu Moge < Sheng Nuzhen / Shu Nuzhen ; Sumo Moge Qidan	Tujue Kirghiz Huiqi - Huigu	Qiang < Dangxiang / Tuyuhun / Tufan
Song Yuan	960-1279 1261-1360	Mongols < Kiyat / Tatars / Merkit / Naiman / Kereit / Ongguts Xiliao (Black Qidan) Sheng Nuzhen		Tufan Tufan
Ming Qing	1368-1644 1644-1911	Mongols < Khalkhas / Oirats Nuzhen < Jianzhou Nuzhen (Manchu) / Haixi Nuzhen / Yeren Nuzhen		Tufan Tibetans

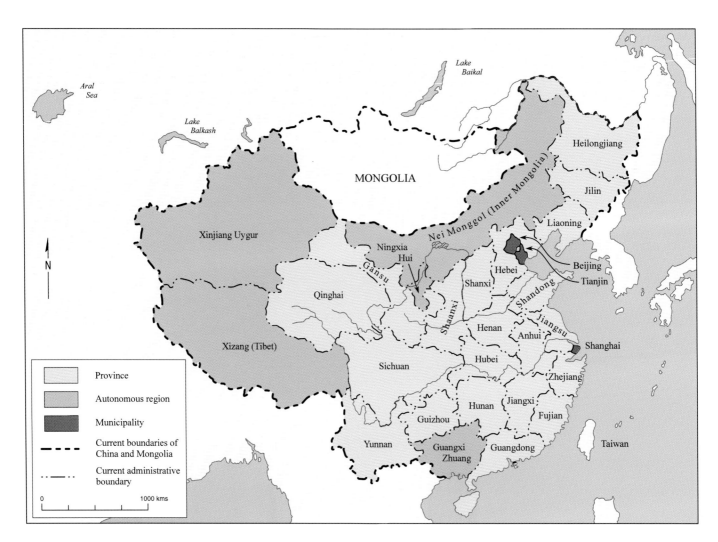

Figure 1   Political Divisions of People's Republic of China, 1994.

of the desert. Today, the former is the state of Mongolia, and the latter is the Inner Mongolian Autonomous Region in China (Figure 1). During the past 45 years, archaeological excavations in Inner Mongolia have uncovered many relics of the nomads of China's northern frontiers. These relics provide evidence of the relationship between the northern nomads and the Han agriculturalists. The oldest finds are the hominid teeth, limb bones, and stone implements at Yinchuan, on the western edge of the bend of the Huang He, and along the Salawusu River on the Ordos Plateau (Wu, 1986, p.39). The name Hetao Man (or Ordos Man) is used to refer to these human fossils, which are dated at approximately 40,000 years ago, roughly contemporary to the Liujiang Man and Qilinshan Man in the Guangxi Zhuang Autonomous Region. The Hetao Man, Liujiang Man, and Qilinshan Man are considered to be modern man, Homo sapiens, who started to replace the Dingcun Man and Maba Man, comparable to the Homo Neanderthalensis in Germany. The Hetao Man on the Ordos Plateau were gatherers and hunters of wild game such as boars, bison and deer, and made simple tools of stone and bones, including scrapers, hand-axes, and choppers. These were utilized for skinning animals and cutting meat. Their culture is referred to as the Palaeolithic Culture (Old Stone Age) on the Ordos Plateau (Figure 2).

There was probably a climatic change approximately 10,000 years ago; and the climate grew warmer and wetter during the subsequent millennia (Kessler, 1993, p.27). The soil formed from the loess (the fine, yellow dust from the Gobi Desert) was very fertile if watered, and easy to work with simple wooden or stone implements. At various archaeological sites in the southern part of present-day Inner Mongolia, farming tools dated from about 5000 to 3000 B.C. have been found. These include stone axes and adzes for cutting and shaping, querns for grinding grain, and other simple farming tools. Their use marked the beginning of the Neolithic Culture, which, by definition, saw the beginning of arable farming. The Hongshan culture was the most significant of the Neolithic types in Inner Mongolia, developing and flourishing from about 4500 to 3000 B.C. on the Laoha and the Xilamulun, tributaries of the Xiliao River. The people of the Hongshan culture, living near the southern border of present day Inner Mongolia, had a well-developed agricultural economy and advanced techniques of polishing, drilling and carving, which they used to manufacture painted pottery and carved jade artifacts (Kessler, 1993, pp.29-31). They were contemporaries of the agriculturalists of the Yangshao Culture (the Painted Pottery Culture), in the middle and upper reaches of the Huang He in North China.

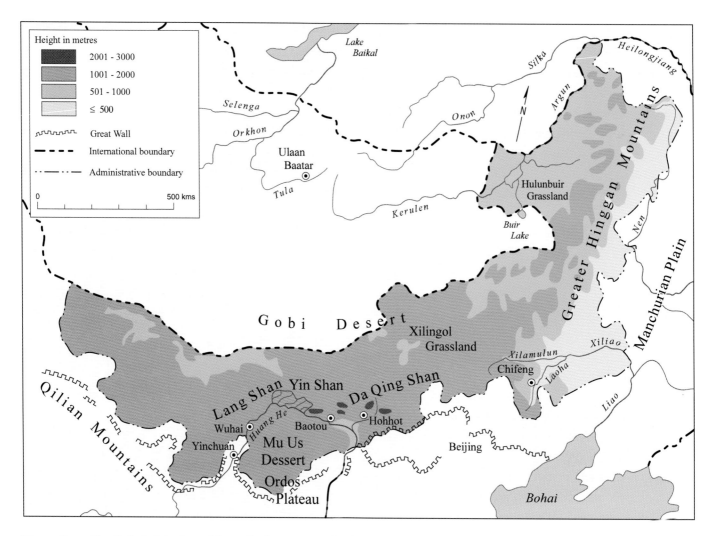

Figure 2   The Relief of the Inner Mongolia Autonomous Region.

Since 1960, Chinese archaeologists have discovered strata of early bronze culture at Xiajiadian, a village near the City of Chifeng, Inner Mongolia. Two layers of bronze culture were identified, namely the lower Xiajiadian layer (c.2000 to c.1600 B.C.), and the upper Xiajiadian layer (c.1100 to c.600 B.C.) (Wu, 1986, p.40). The Lower Xiajiadian Culture, dominated by farming, was closely connected with the Shang culture of the Han people (c.1766 to c.1122 B.C.). There was probably another climatic change in Inner Mongolia, around 1500 B.C. (Kessler, 1993, p.35). A drier and colder climate appears to have made arable farming difficult and forced some of the people of the Lower Xiajiadian Culture to migrate southward to the Huang He Delta. Those remaining may have abandoned farming and taken up hunting and herding on the grassland, becoming the nomads of the Upper Xiajidian Culture known as the *Hu* in Chinese history. The Chinese used Hu as a general term for all the northern pastoral nomads who fought on horseback (Lattimore, 1963, p.1).

Two distinct civilizations, based on different economies, had emerged in China's northern frontiers by the eleventh century B.C. The agriculturalists who claimed to be descendants of the Yellow Emperor, created an advanced civilization in the Wei valley of the Huang He, and started the Western Zhou Dynasty (c.1122 to 771 B.C.). They constituted the present day Han Chinese. The Hu, comprised of many nomadic tribes herding and hunting on the Mongolian grassland, did not have a written language nor permanent dwellings, cities, or well-organized governments. In their historic records, the Han people referred to them as "barbarians" and tried to exert political control over them through cultural influence and military conquest. In contrast, the nomads frequently invaded the Han agriculturalists, considering them as slaves to their lands who could not survive once they left their protective niches. Unlike the farmers, the mobile nomads could constantly look for more fertile land. These two groups of people despised each other and constantly fought. Throughout Chinese history, their relationship has been a cyclic pattern of conflicts, warfare, alliances, and peaceful coexistence.

LAND AND PEOPLE

Inner Mongolia is China's third largest autonomous region after Xinjiang and Tibet, covering an area of nearly 1.2 million sq. km., or about one-ninth of China's total territory. It occupies the southern rim of the Mongolian Plateau which lies between 800 and 1,300 metres above sea level. The northern border of the crescent-shaped Inner Mongolia is dominated by the Gobi Desert, which is a broad basin-like depression dotted with salt marshes and inland drainage. Away from the desert core is an arc of semi-arid deserts and grassland. Further to the south is another arc of low mountains which constitute the eastern and southern borders of the Plateau. Its upturned eastern edge is the Greater Hinggan Mountains which rise, in many places, above 2,000 metres, and plunge down to the Nen river valley which is part of the Manchurian Plain. Although these high ranges appear as a line of low hills from the west, they look like a high dissected escarpment from the east. Along the southern rim of the Plateau are the Yin Shan Ranges which are 2,000 metres above sea-level. The Ranges consist of a series of low mountains such as the Da Qing Shan and Lang Shan (Sun, 1957, pp. 5-6). South of the Yin Shan

Ranges is the Huang He. Here the river, descending from Qinghai Province, flows northward, eastward, and then southward, in the shape of an inverted letter "U". This section of the river is known as the loop of the Huang He. On the northern side of the loop is the Hetao Plain which consists of the Houtao Plain east of Baotou, and the Hohhot Plain. Within the loop is the Ordos Plateau at an altitude of about 1,000 metres, where the Mu Us Desert is located. Unlike the Gobi Desert which is "swept clean" of fine sediments, the Mu Us Desert is able to supply vast amounts of sand and silt (Cressey, 1960, p. 399).

Inner Mongolia's climate is continental, with extremes of seasonal and diurnal temperatures. Its winter is long and severe, lasting from November to March. The mean January temperature ranges from -28°C in the north to -9°C in the south. Cold, strong winds frequently sweep over the region, drying up the soil, and blowing so much dust high into the atmosphere that the sky may be darkened, even during the day. The short summer lasts from June to August, and the mean July temperature varies from 18°C in the north to 24°C in the south. There are only 110 to 150 annual frost-free days. Rainfall is sparse, variable and precarious, and droughts occur almost yearly. Annual precipitation decreases from about 400 mm in the southeast to 200 mm in the northwest, with most of the rainstorms from June to August. Torrential rains often cause mud flows which destroy vegetation and crops on plains and in valleys.

Because of its arid, cold climate, and high altitude, the Mongolian Plateau is by no means a hospitable terrain. Cultivation is difficult, if not impossible. Temperate grasslands, desert-steppes, and arid deserts dominate. In 1986, Inner Mongolia, having a pasture land of 880,000 sq km, was the leading animal husbandry region of China's five most important pastoral regions (Deng, 1987, p.77). Very fertile grasslands such as the Hulunbuir and the Xilingol are located in the eastern part of Inner Mongolia (Ren, 1985, pp.347-348). The desert-steppes, which are composed of small bunch grasses and half-shrubs, are situated mainly in the western, or on the Ordos Plateau. Livestock herding is by far the most common economic activity of the autonomous region. About half the herds are sheep and goats, and the rest are cattle, horses, camels, and other stock. Sheep are less adaptable than goats, and are more numerous in the wetter and more fertile steppes of eastern Mongolia. Topography and climate combine to restrict farming to the Nen River Plain, the Xiliao Plain, the Hetao Plain, and a few oases with adequate rainfall or available irrigation. In such regions, the major crops are spring wheat, kaoliang (sorghum), and millet.

Historically, the Mongolian Plateau was the heartland of many pastoral nomads such as the Xiongnu, the Ruanruan (Rouran), the Tujue, and the Huiqi. They hunted and herded, and migrated constantly in search of good pastures and water supply. As a result, unlike the Han people, they could not settle down in one area long enough to develop a strong lineage. Nor could they establish a state like the monarchy of the Han people because they needed the wide expanses of the plateau for hunting game and raising flocks of sheep, goats, horses and other animals. Occupying a large geographical area, the northern nomads spoke many dialects and languages, but they shared numerous common words and phrases because of inter-marriages and intermixture during migration. Hence, communication was not a serious problem, although there was no written language until the thirteenth century A.D.

The precarious climatic regime of the Mongolian arid-steppes frequently caused droughts and other natural disasters which led to armed conflicts over the possession of flocks, well-watered land or fertile grassland between one tribe and another. The cold and dry climate of the plateau also made it impossible to grow food grains and other agricultural produce. If the nomads wanted these products, they had to get them either through trade, or conquest of the land which produced them. After they crossed the Yin Shan Mountains from the Mongolian Plateau, the northern nomads riding on their horses could descend quickly to raid the Chinese agriculturalists in their fertile valley, yet they also could retreat rapidly if they encountered strong resistance. Their striking power was amazing. Standing up on iron stirrups hanging down from the saddle of the horse, a rider could use bow and arrow to attack the peasant foot soldiers at a distance.

The Han agriculturalists, on the other hand, not only defended their fields against the invasions of the steppe nomads, but also tried to occupy their fertile grasslands to convert them into arable land. As a result, many forests and grasslands of the Mongols' homeland were devastated. For example, in the mid-1700s, the southern mountainous rim of the Mongolian Plateau was covered with forests and rich pastures. As cultivation expanded into these areas, "all the trees were grubbed up, the forests disappeared from the hills, the prairies were cleared by means of fire, and the new cultivators set busily to work in exhausting the fecundity of the soil" (Cressey, 1933, p.278). The Mongols were forced to move further north to look for new grasslands for their herds.

The vast, flat plateau which had virtually no physical barriers, was well suited to the Mongol nomads who needed mobility in warfare and good pasture. Riding their horses, they could move very quickly and easily on the level grasslands and semi-arid steppes. Traditionally they spent much of their time on horseback and seldom walked because they had to move constantly with their flocks to seek water and better grazing. From childhood, both men and women spent most of their days in the saddle. They were so inseparable from their horses that Sima Qian, a famous Chinese historian in the Han Dynasty, called their country a "state on horseback," meaning a state continuously on the move (Jagchid and Hyer, 1979, p.5).

Similar to the early American cowboys, the steppe pastoralists were self-reliant and omnicompetent because of their individual outdoor activities. Their bravery and aggressive energies were valuable in the control of their flocks, the pursuit of wild game, or the annihilation of rivals. They did not wander indiscriminately but recognized group rights in pastures and moved along a fixed seasonal route from winter camp to summer pasture and back to winter camp (Krader, 1955, p.302). They would fight for pastures and over routes from pasture to pasture, if their rights were violated. Since there were no physical features to define the boundaries of pasture and the routes, constant disputes over ownership often led to warfare among these herdsmen-hunters-warriors of the steppe.

The Mongolian nomads, because of their constant migration, had to be very mobile and lived in yurts, which could be assembled, dismantled, and packed easily and quickly. (A yurt is a cylindrical-shaped tent with a domed roof which is supported internally by a collapsible latticework of wood, and covered on the outside with skins or felt). In addition to their sturdy "Mongol ponies," the Mongols also used cattle and camels to pull wooden carts, onto which all their household belongings, including yurts, were loaded.

The traditional way of life, based on herding on the Mongolian Plateau, changed rapidly in the early twentieth century. Modernization and Mongolian nationalism began with the expansion of the Russian, Chinese, and Japanese spheres of influence in the 1920s. After the establishment of the People's Republic of China in 1949, the landscape and economy of Inner Mongolia was greatly altered by the new government's policy of industrialization. Factories engaged in food-processing and leather-making were built in Hohhot (formerly Kueisui), and iron-smelting and steel-making plants were set up in Baotou. Although pastoral pursuits continue to dominate the lives of many Mongolians, agriculture, mining, manufacturing, and tourism also have come to play an increasing economic role.

Plate 4 *A Kirghiz Yurt*

THE DONGHU AND XIONGNU IN THE WARRING STATES PERIOD, 475-221 B.C.

Two groups of northern nomads were identified during the Western Zhou Dynasty (c. 1122-771 B.C.), namely, the Di living in the area north of the Wei valley, and the Quan Rong roaming on the grassland to west of the valley (Figure 3). These two tribes had been competing for land with the Han people since the early twelfth century B.C. (Lu, 1976, Vol. 2, pp. 379-380). In 770 B.C., the Quan Rong succeeded in occupying the Wei River valley and forced Emperor Zhou Pingwang to move his capital from Haojing near present day Xi'an to Luoyi located at what is now Luoyang (Lo, 1956, pp.92-3). This event marked the beginning of the Eastern Zhou Dynasty (770-249 B.C.).

During the seventh century B.C., more than a hundred vassal states were established by feudal lords who contended for land and people in North China. They constantly fought amongst themselves, conquering other states and in turn being conquered. By the beginning of the Period of the Warring States (475-221 B.C.), only seven major states remained, namely, the Yan, Zhao, Wei, Qin, Qi, Han, and Chu. There were also two major northern tribes, namely the Donghu and the Xiongnu. The Donghu was a loose confederation of Tungusic-speaking tribes, living on grassland in the Xiliao River valley. The Xiongnu (the Huns) were another group of nomads roaming the grassland between the Gobi Desert and the loop of the Huang He. The Xiongnu leader was Touman Chanyu (Chanyu is a term for a Xiongnu chieftain) who was one of the brilliant chieftains before the birth of Genghis Khan. He led the Xiongnu to approach the height of their power during the early Han Dynasty and was described in Chinese historical records as

a tall, deep-chested man of powerful frame mounted on a diminutive pony of the pure white strain which only the nomad nobility might ride. His long robe falls below the tops of his high boots. He wears a turban-like cap and a full beard; and his features are dark and implacable. His eyes stare upwards as if in commune with the supreme god of sky and sun. He holds his loose rein in his left hand, and his bow in his right. From his saddle is slung a quiver filled with arrows. In such a figure the jackal-voiced, tiger-hearted emperor had a redoubtable opponent (Legg, 1971, p. 83).

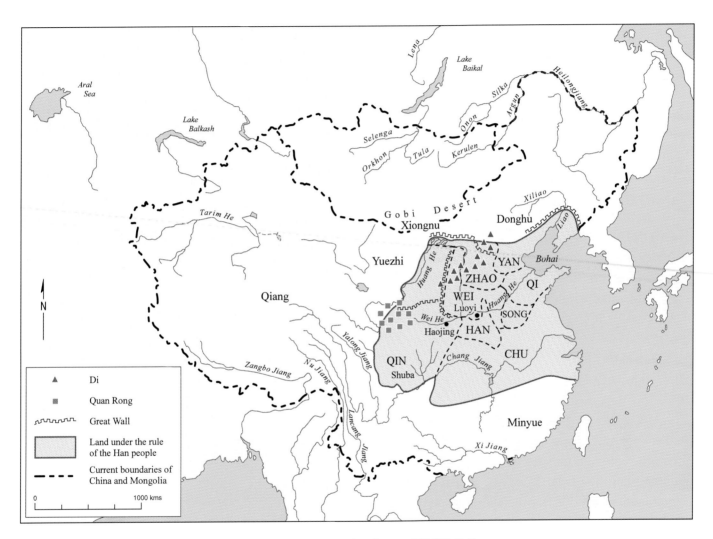

Figure 3 The Donghu and Xiongnu in the Period of the Warring States, 475-221 B.C.

The Donghu and Xiongnu constantly invaded North China and forced the states of Yan, Zhao and Qin to build fortification walls along their northern borders.

In the second century B.C., the Emperor Qin Shi Huang united the Han people through conquest, and established the Qin Dynasty (221-207 B.C.). After he drove the Donghu back to their homeland, he turned his attention to the Xiongnu. In 215 B.C. he instructed his general, Mengtian, to lead 300,000 soldiers to drive Touman Chanyu and his hordes out of the loop of the Huang He and pursue them across the Gobi Desert. In order to stabilize his northern frontiers, Emperor Qin started to construct the Great Wall. This he did by connecting all the individual walls of previous states. The Great Wall followed the highlands of the southern rim of the Mongolian Plateau from the Greater Hinggan to the north-eastern corner of the loop of the Huang He. In addition to being a line of military fortification, the Great Wall also marked a climatic transition, dividing the lands to the south, which received monsoonal rains, from the Gobi and Ordos Deserts to the north, roughly marking the limit of interior drainage (Cressey, 1932, pp.273-275). For many years it functioned as a divide between pastoral nomadism in the north and arable farming in the south.

Plate 5   *A Mongolian Lama of the Yellow Sect*

THE XIONGNU EMPIRE IN THE HAN DYNASTY, 206 B.C.-A.D. 220

After he was defeated by Mengtian, Touman started to form alliances with his steppe neighbours and seized pasture lands from weaker nomads (Legg, 1971, pp.88-90). With the help of Maodun, his eldest son, he had succeeded in building up a strong Xiongnu empire across the Mongolian Plateau by the end of the third century (Sun, 1951, p.10). He led the Xiongnu in invading the Donghu and occupying their pasture lands. The Donghu tribes were scattered: the Shiwei fled northward to the Greater Hinggan Mountains, the Xianbei moved to the northern bank of the Xiliao River, while the Wuhuan retreated to the Laoha River (Figure 4).

After the Xiongnu broke up the Donghu confederation, Maodun directed his forces to the west, and drove out the Yuezhi, an Indo-European-speaking people, from their homeland in present day Gansu Province to Afghanistan. By the beginning of the Han Dynasty (206 B.C.-A.D.220), the Xiongnu had founded the first nomadic empire on the Asian steppes. Its vast territory spread from present day Liaoning Province through Inner Mongolia into Xinjiang Uygur Autonomous Region. Although it did not have defined political boundaries on the vast grassland and deserts, the Xiongnu Empire lasted for nearly 300 years.

Border wars between the Xiongnu and the Han people were almost incessant throughout the Han Dynasty. Contemporary Chinese historians described the customs and the military strategy of the Xiongnu in detail. For example, Pan Ku, a famous historian of the Han Dynasty, wrote that the Xiongnu:

raise a variety of animals, most of which are horses, cattle, and sheep....The Xiongnu do not have any written language. When life becomes difficult, all men are taught the art of warfare, preparing ardently for the launching of attacks ....They rely on bows and arrows if the enemy is at a distance and switch to knives and spears in close combat....They attack when the moon is large and bright, and withdraw when it becomes small and dim....On the battlefield all Xiongnu soldiers fought valiantly for their own material ends, upon which they converge like hungry vultures. Upon a setback, however, they disintegrate quickly and disperse like flying clouds. Their favourite strategy is to entice

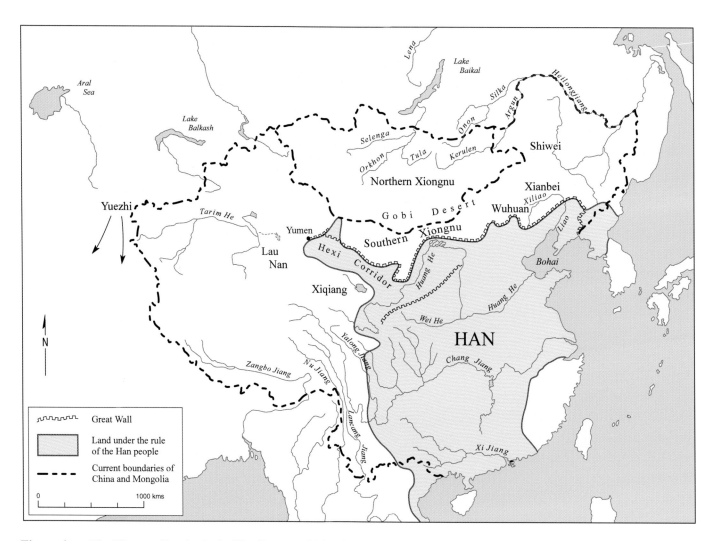

Figure 4   The Xiongnu Empire in the Han Dynasty, 206 B.C. - A.D. 220.

their enemy to a pre-arranged place and then encircle him. After a battle, the warrior who brings home the body of a dead comrade will inherit all the latter's worldly possession (Li, 1967, p.212).

Ch'ao Ts'o, another Chinese historian of the Han Dynasty, gave a detailed account of the Xiongnu way of life and military strategy, suggesting methods of dealing with Xiongnu invasion. He wrote that:

the northern barbarians eat meat, drink milk, and wear animal furs and skins. They have no fields, houses, or cities. Like birds and beasts, they move from place to place and stop only when they find water and good grass...

The difference between large and small countries is not only a difference in military strength but also a difference in policies and in the strategy of defence. The normal course for a small country to follow is to admit its inferiority and be subservient to a country of great strength. If it wishes to attack a larger and stronger country, it will have to make alliances with other small countries. However, as far as China is concerned, her basic policy is to use barbarians to fight barbarians....

The Xiongnu horses are superior to those of China if the terrain is rugged, bisected by steep mountains and deep streams. Their riders can easily outdo their Chinese counterparts when maneuvering on dangerous roads and narrow passes, and compared with the Chinese, can shoot better while galloping at full speed. The Xiongnu soldiers can stand the elements better, become tired less easily, and can fight for much longer time without water or food.

If the terrain is level and easy to traverse, the Chinese light-chariots and cavalry elite can easily rout a Xiongnu force....The Chinese bow is stronger, can cover a longer distance.... In group combat, the Chinese can take full advantage of their strong armour, sharp knife, effective bow and arrows. The Chinese arrows, coming from a strong bow, can easily penetrate the leather armour or wooden plate of a Xiongnu soldiers... (Li, 1967, pp.213-4).

Using "barbarians" to fight against "barbarians" had always been the strategy of the Han people when dealing with the northern nomads. The Han Emperor was also advised that thousands of the "barbarians" who had surrendered and been assimilated into the Han society should be given strong armour, tough clothing, powerful bows and sharp arrows, and stationed in rugged terrain, because they had habits and skills that were similar to the Xiongnu's. When battles were to be fought on plains, the Chinese cavalrymen and light chariots should be used.

Emperor Han Wudi and his successors adopted these military strategies to deal with the Xiongnu, and eventually succeeded in destroying their power south of the Gobi Desert in 119 B.C. Having driven the Xiongnu back into central Mongolia, the Han emperors extended the Great Wall from the loop of the Huang He to Yumen in order to protect the Hexi Corridor through which the Silk Road passed. The decline of the Xiongnu power was hastened further by internal dissension which in 60 B.C. resulted in the split of the Xiongnu into two factions: the Northern Xiongnu and Southern Xiongnu.

Throughout the second century B.C. the Southern Xiongnu had been constantly invading China. To appease the Xiongnu the Han Emperors used either military offensives or title grants and gifts. Emperor Han Wendi, for example, wrote in 162 B.C. to the Xiongnu chief that:

Since your country is located in the north where winter is long and cold, we have agreed to present to you a sizable amount of grain, gold, silk, and many other items each year as gifts. Now that peace has prevailed throughout the world, how wonderful it is to see people rejoice in it (Li, 1967, p. 219).

The Han emperors also tried to secure a peaceful frontier by matrimonial alliances. In 33 B.C., for example, Emperor Han Yuandi (48-33 B.C.) sent Wang Zhaojun, a beautiful lady-in-waiting, to Mongolia to marry Huhanye Chanyu, a Southern Xiongnu chieftain. This marriage tie proved to be an effective means of appeasing the Xiongnu because it helped keep peace in China's northern frontiers for over fifty years.

Plate 6   *The Ruined City of Jiaohe Near Turpan on the Silk Road*

THE FIVE NOMADIC TRIBES IN THE EASTERN JIN DYNASTY, 217-420

The northern tribes constantly invaded China throughout the third and fourth centuries A.D. In 304, Liu Yuan, a Xiongnu noble, established the Kingdom of Han in the south-western part of present day Shanxi Province. He was succeeded by Liu Yao who renamed his state the Kingdom of Former Zhao, and rebelled against the Jin Dynasty. His forces overran Luoyang, the capital of Jin, and forced Emperor Jin Yuandi (317-322) to remove his capital to Jiankang (present day Nanjing); hence the Eastern Jin Dynasty (317-420) began in Central and South China (Figure 5). Encouraged by the successful revolt of the Xiongnu, four other tribes, namely the Di, Jie, Xianbei, and Qiang, also took up arms to throw off the yoke of the Han people, and set up their own states (Qian, 1977, Vol. 1, pp.186-192). By the beginning of the fifth century, a total of 13 small states had been established in North China by the five northern tribes (Table 2). In Chinese history their occupation of North China was referred to as the *Wuhu Luanhua* (meaning Five Nomadic Tribes Throwing China Into Disorder).

In Chinese history, the Period of the Northern and Southern Dynasties (420-589) started with the es-
tablishment of the Liu Song Dynasty (420-479) in South China by Liu Yu, a military officer. In 420 he dethroned Emperor Jin Gongdi, and ended the Eastern Jin Dynasty. His dynasty was soon followed by a succession of three similar short-lived dynasties, namely the Qi, Liang, and Chen dynasties.

In North China, Tuoba Gui, the leader of the Tuoba Xianbei (Tabgach), set up the state of Northern Wei (386-534), and proclaimed himself emperor at his capital, Pingcheng (near present day Datong), in 386. His successors subjugated other contending tribes, and unified North China under their rule in the Northern Wei Dynasty (386-535), followed by the Eastern Wei, Western Wei, Northern Qi and Northern Zhou dynasties.

Throughout the period of the Northern and Southern Dynasties, the nomadic tribes moved back and forth across China's northern frontiers, and intermingled more frequently with the Han people. In this way many of them became assimilated into the Han culture.

While China was occupied by the northern tribes, another groups of nomads rose to power on the Mongolian Plateau. They were Turkic-speaking and known as the Ruanruan (Rouran). The title "khan", borne by

Figure 5   The Distribution of Nomadic Tribes in North China During the Eastern Jin Dynasty, 217-420.

their chiefs, made its first appearance around 500 (Hoang, 1990, p.104). The Ruanruan subdued other tribes on the Mongolian Plateau, and established an empire to the north of Northern Wei. Their empire was overthrown in the mid-sixth century by the Tujue, another group of Turkic-speaking nomadic tribes in Mongolia. The title, "khan" was later perpetuated by the Tujue chiefs and their conquerors.

Table 2   Name and Location of the 16 States, 304-443

Ethnic Group	Name of State	Approximate Location
Xiongnu	Han (Former Zhao)	Hebei-Shanxi border
Xiongnu	Northern Liang	Northern Gansu
Xiongnu	Xia	Ordos Plateau
Xianbei	Former Yan	Huanghe delta
Xianbei	Later Yan	Northern Hebei
Xianbei	Western Qin	Central Gansu
Xianbei	Southern Liang	Central Gansu
Xianbei	Southern Yan	Shangdong
Di	Cheng Han	Sichuan
Di	Former Qin	North of Wei River
Di	Later Liang	Central Gansu
Jie	Later Zhao	Shanxi-Hebei border
Qiang	Later Qin	Wei River valley
Han	Former Liang	Central Gansu
Han	Western Liang	Northern Gansu
Han	Northern Yan	Southern Liaoning

(See Glossary, p. 70).

THE TUJUE EMPIRE IN THE
SUI AND TANG DYNASTIES, 581-907

North and South China were united again under the rule of the Han people during the Sui Dynasty (581-617). The Sui Emperor immediately tried to establish good relationships with the nomadic tribes by marrying daughters of the Imperial family to their chiefs, or, if this failed, he would send military forces to fight against them. By this time the Tujue had formed a loose Tujue Empire across the Mongolian Plateau. They were divided into two branches: the Eastern Tujue living in the area drained by the Orkhon River, and the Western Tujue in the present day Xinjiang Uygur Autonomous Region and the area south of Lake Balkash (Figure 6). During the 29 years of the Sui Dynasty, the Tujue had been raiding China constantly. They even assisted Li Yuan to overthrow the Sui Dynasty and establish the Tang Dynasty (618-907).

Throughout the seventh century, the Tang emperors had been trying to pacify their frontier peoples. Initially, the Tang emperor successfully subjugated the three Tungusic-speaking or Mongolian-speaking tribes in North-eastern China, namely, the Mengwu Shiwei, Qidan (Khitan), and Moge (Lo, 1956, Vol. 1, p.290). The term Menggu (the Mongols) first appeared in the Tang Dynasty where it was used to describe two major groups: the Mengwu Shiwei and the Tatars. At that time, the Mengwu Shiwei were a small unimportant group of steppe herdsmen who hunted and raised herds on the grassland between the upper reaches of the Onon and Kerulen rivers. The Tatars pastured their herds on the grassland north of the Yin Shan Ranges. The Qidan, probably the descendants of mixed Xianbei and Xiongnu, lived on the banks of the Xiliao and Laoha rivers where they grew crops and reared animals. Both the Menggu and Qidan shared the territory which is in present day Inner Mongolia with the Moge (the ancestors of the Manchu). The Moge were divided into two major branches: the Heishui Moge and Sumo Moge. The Heishui Moge, living in the forests of the Lower Heilongjiang, pursued a mixed economy of forest hunting, reindeer herding, fishing, and arable farming. The Sumo Moge, occupying the delta of the Liao River, were basically agriculturalists. In 713 they founded the Pohai state, which covered the south of what is now Liaoning Province, and the northern part of present day North Korea.

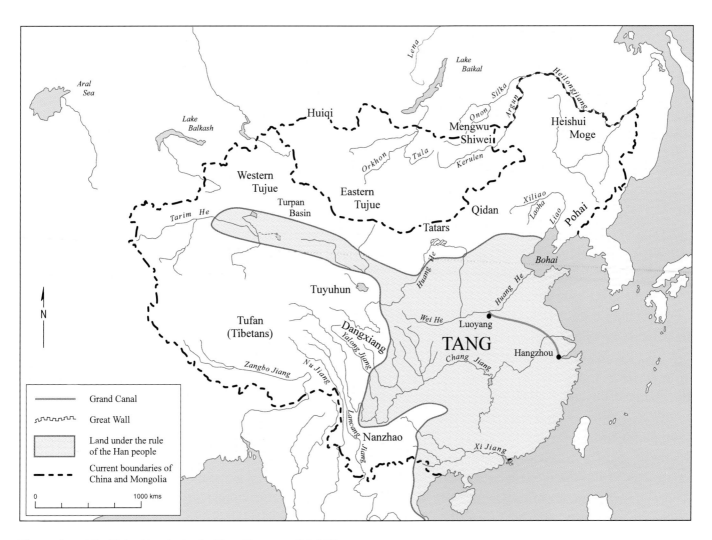

Figure 6   The Tujue Empire in the Tang Dynasty, 618-907

In 626, Xieli Khan of the Eastern Tujue invaded China, and threatened Chang'an, capital of the Tang (Bai, 1982, p.212). Emperor Tang Taizong (627-649) sent Li Jing and other generals to lead a massive counter-attack in 629. After Xieli Khan was captured in 630, the Eastern Tujue were subdued and pledged allegiance to the Tang. In 651, the Western Tujue, led by Shaboluo Khan rebelled against the Tang. Accordingly, in 657, Emperor Tang Gaozong (650-683) sent Su Dingfang and other generals to invade the Western Tujue (Lo, 1956, Vol. 1, pp. 215-6). With the help of the Huiqi (the Uygurs), the Tang generals captured Shaboluo Khan and subdued the Western Tujue, toppling the Tujue Empire.

The Huiqi were initially an insignificant group of nomads living in the northern part of the Tujue Empire. They rose to power after they formed an alliance with the Tang Emperor. By the mid-eighth century, they had established a semi-nomadic Uygur Empire in the present day Xinjiang Uygur Autonomous Region, and controlled the Silk Road (Zhang, 1954, p.26). Many of them were later converted to the faith of Islam which followed the caravan routes from Persia. Through the Huiqi, between 628 and 651 during the Tang Dynasty, Islam began to diffuse into China (Shi, 1957, p.418).

For many years, the Uygurs joined forces with the Tang to fight against the Qiang or Xiqiang, who were Tibetan-speaking pastoralists occupying what is present day Qingzang Plateaux (Qinghai and Tibetan Plateaux). The Qiang were divided into three major branches, namely, the Tuyuhun, Dangxiang (the Tanguts), and Tufan (Tibetans). In about 620, Songtsen Gampo (?-650), the seventh chief of a tribe called Sibu, completed the political unification of the Tufan and established the Tibetan Empire (c.620 to c.820) (Tanjun Ranopanza, 1993, pp.7-8). In 641, Emperor Tang Taizong, in the face of a threat of Tufan invasion, adopted an appeasement policy by marrying his daughter, Princess Wencheng, to Songtsen Gampo (Sinha, 1964, p.25). The Princess took Buddhist scriptures and images with her to Tibet, and introduced Chinese knowledge and techniques in agriculture, handicrafts, buildings, and medicine to the Tibetan people (Wang and Suo, 1984, p.15). In 641, she also built Jokhang Monastery at Pagor Street in Lhasa. After the death of Songtsen Gampo in 650, the matrimonial alliance with the Tang Dynasty collapsed, and intermittent fighting between the Tufan and the Han broke out. In 710, Emperor Tang Zhongzong (684-710) tried to enlist the loyalty of the Tufan again by marrying Princess Jincheng to the Tufan King, Tride Tsugtsen (704-754). The Princess also brought with her many artisans, silk fabrics, and Confucian classics to Tufan. The two princesses, therefore, played an important role in introducing Chinese culture and technology into Tufan.

In the early ninth century, the Kirghiz, the Turkic-speaking nomads in the western part of present day Mongolia, rose to power. In 846, they drove the Uygurs out of Mongolia, and broke up the Uygur Empire. It was at about this time that Tibet Lamaism began to diffuse to Mongolia.

Plate 8   *A Lama Monastery in a Village Near Hohhot*

THE EMERGENCE OF A QIDAN STATE IN THE FIVE DYNASTIES PERIOD, 907-960

After the collapse of the Tujue and Uygur empires, the northern tribes broke up, and again began to fight. Some of the Uygurs who had been driven out of Mongolia by the Kirghiz escaped to the Turpan Basin where they established the Huigu state. Meanwhile, in 901, the Qidan rose to power again under the leadership of Yelu Abaoji. He established a new Qidan state and called it the Liao (907-1125) (Figure 7). His forces marched east to conquer the Pohai state in 926, then moved north to break up the confederation of the Heishui Moge. Hence, the Heishui Moge was split into two branches: the Shu Nuzhen in the south, and the Sheng Nuzhen in the north. The former was absorbed by the Liao and the latter accepted Liao's overlordship.

While the Qidan were building up a strong state, the central government of the Tang Dynasty had been much weakened by the increasing power of the frontier commanders who were in charge of the country's military regions. Towards the end of the ninth century, these frontier commanders disobeyed the central government and fought among themselves. Eventually, in 907 Zhu Wen, who was in charge of the military region in present day Henan and Anhui provinces, usurped the throne, and established the Later Liang (907-923), the first dynasty of the Five Dynasties (907-960) in North China. It lasted only 17 years and was replaced by the Later Tang (923-936). Then Shi Jingtang, another frontier commander, sought the help of the Liao forces and succeeded in overthrowing the Later Tang, establishing the Later Jin Dynasty (936-947). In return for the help of the Qidan, he ceded 16 border prefectures (Yanyun Shiliu Zhou) in the northern part of present day Shanxi and Hebei provinces to the Liao.

While in North China one dynasty was being rapidly replaced by another, a military junta was busy in partitioning other parts of China, setting up small kingdoms (Qian, 1977, Vol. 2, pp.378-379). Except for Northern Han, all these were established in Central or South China (Table 3). Spatially they often corresponded with physical or economic regions. For example, the Shu state occupied the Sichuan Basin, the Nan Ping state was established in the middle reach of the Chang Jiang basin, and the Nan Han state covered what is now Guangdong Province and the Guangxi Zhuang Autonomous Region.

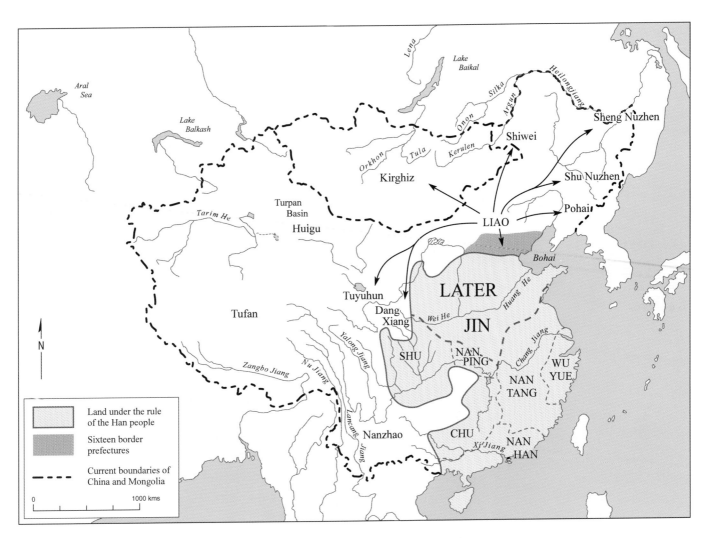

Figure 7   The Expansion of the Liao State in the Period of Five Dynasties, 907-960

Table 3 The Five Dynasties and Ten Kingdoms, 907-960

Five Dynasties in North China	*Ten Kingdoms in Central or South China*
Later Liang (907-923)	Wu (920-937)
	Wu Yue (907-978)
	Nan Han (907-971)
	Chu (907-951)
	Qian Shu (907-925)
	Min (909-945)
Later Tang (923-936)	Nan Ping (924-963)
Later Jin (936-946)	Hou Shu (934-965)
Later Han (947-950)	Nan Tang (937-975)
Later Zhou (951-960)	Bei Han (951-979)

(See Glossary, p. 71)

Plate 9   *A Khalkha Rider on a Typical Mongolian Pony*

THE TRIUMVIRATE OF THE QIDAN, DANGXIANG AND HAN PEOPLE IN THE NORTHERN SONG DYNASTY, 960-1127

Throughout the eleventh and twelfth centuries, the Northern Song Dynasty co-existed with the State of Liao (916-1125) established by the Qidan, and the State of Xixia (1038-1227) established by the Dangxiang. By the tenth century, the Liao had become a strong state and defeated Emperor Song Taizong (976-997) four times in his attempt to take back the 16 border prefectures. In 1004, the Liao launched a massive invasion of China. In exchange for peace, Emperor Song Zhenzong (998-1022) agreed to make an annual contribution of 100,000 taels of silver, and 200,000 bolts of silk to the Liao (Lo, 1956, Vol. 1, p.295). Forty years later, the Liao threatened to invade again, and forced Emperor Song Renzong (1023-1063) to add another 100,000 taels of silver and 100,000 bolts of silk to his annual tributes. By the eleventh century, the Liao state extended from north-eastern China across Inner Mongolia to the loop of the Huang He (Figure 8). Its administration was organized to include five capitals: Shangjing (the Upper Capital) near present day Balinzuo Banner; Zhongjing (the Middle Capital) near Ningcheng; Dongjing (the Eastern Capital) at Liaoyang; Xijing (the Western Capital) at Datong, and Nanjing (the Southern Capital) at Beijing (Figure 9).

According to some scholars, there is a close connection between the Qidan of the Liao and the evolution of nomadic tribes on the Mongolian Plateau, which were to fuse together to form the Mongol Empire in the twelfth century (Lattimore, 1963, p.4). At this time Mongolia was invaded by the Qidan from the east rather than from the south by the Han, as had been commonplace. The Qidan drive moved different Mongol tribes across the Plateau to Central Asia, and opened the way for the expansion of the Mongol language at the expense of Turkic. Henceforth, the east-west penetration of the Qidan across Mongolia was much greater than the south-north penetration of the Han into Mongolia. The medieval European term for the country of Qidan was "Cathay" (Kitai), which is still used by the Russians and some central Asian peoples for "China" (Fairbank, 1978, p.123). In his book about his travel to China, Marco Polo also called it Cathay. The term Cathay was mistaken for "China" partly because the Europeans in those days did not know much about Asia, and partly because the Qidan

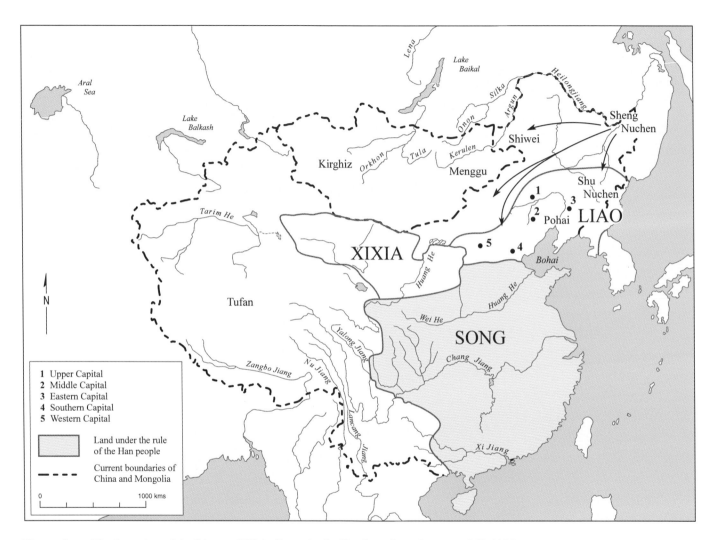

Figure 8   The Location of the Liao and Xixia States in the Northern Song Dynasty, 960-1127.

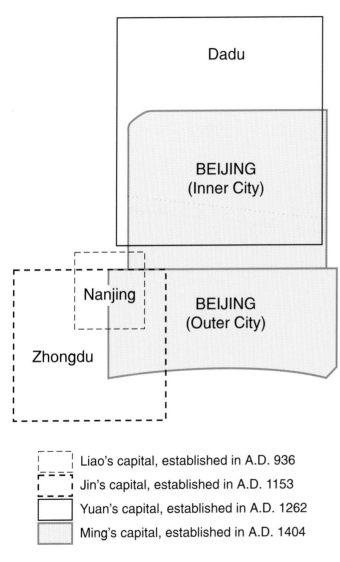

Liao's capital, established in A.D. 936

Jin's capital, established in A.D. 1153

Yuan's capital, established in A.D. 1262

Ming's capital, established in A.D. 1404

Figure 9   Plans of Nanjing, Zhongdu, Dadu, and Beijing.

people were so influential in Central Asia and Europe that Europeans heard more about them than the Han people of China.

The Xixia State was another powerful nomadic state during the Northern Song Dynasty. It occupies present day Gansu Province, Ningxia Hui Autonomous Region, and parts of Shaanxi and Qinghai provinces and the Inner Mongolian Autonomous Region (Gernet, 1989, p.355). Initially the Dangxiang were herdsmen on the Ordos Plateau and were related to the Qiang of the Tang Dynasty. In 1002, they began to spread towards Gansu and western Mongolia, and were enriched by commerce. The governing class of the Xixia consisted of the Dangxiang, who had intermarried with the Tuoba Xianbei (Tabgach), and the Tuyuhun. The population of the Xixia state was very heterogeneous, ranging from the Tuoba Xianbei, Tuyuhun and Tufan to the Uygurs, and even the Han people. The state also covered an area of varied land uses, ranging from semi-deserts and steppes to oases and arable land. Hence, their people were nomadic herdsmen, semi-sedentary herdsmen, caravaneers or farmers. In 1044, unable to check the invasion of the Dangxiang, Emperor Song Renzong (1023-1063) was forced to sign a peace treaty which obliged him to send an annual tribute of 135,00 rolls of silk, 72,000 ounces of silver, and 30,000 pounds of tea to the Xixia state (Gernet, 1989, p.355). The Dangxiang had been much influenced by the Chinese culture. In recent years archaeological excavations have discovered that Xixia had a written language which was based on three styles of Chinese writing, namely the seal characters, the square characters, and the grass text (Lin, 1954, p.308). Near Yinchuan, the capital of the Xixia state, ruins of many palaces, mansions, Buddhist temples, pagodas, and imperial parks also have been discovered (Anon, 1994, p.26). The causes of the end of the Xixia State are still unknown although some historians claim that it was absorbed into the Mongol Empire after Genghis Khan killed the entire imperial family of the state (*China Daily*, Beijing, 7 December 1994).

In far North-eastern China, the Sheng Nuzhen tribes gradually began to move from the lower Heilongjiang to the warmer Songhua River valley. They defeated other tribes during their southward migration, and toward the late eleventh century started to challenge the rule of the Liao.

Plate 10
"The Turtle," a Spectacular Geological Formation South of the Town of Dadal, Province of Khentiy, Mongolia

THE EMERGENCE OF THE JIN AND XILIAO STATES IN THE SOUTHERN SONG DYNASTY, 1127-1279

In 1115, Wanyan Aguda united the Sheng Nuzhen and established the Jin state (1115-1234) (Figure 10). After he launched an attack on the Liao state, other tribes also rebelled against the oppressive rule of the Qidan. In 1125, the Liao state was conquered by the Jin and the Qidan were scattered again. Yclu Dashi, a member of the Liao royal family, escaped to the area south of Lake Balkash, where he set up the Xiliao State (Black Qidan or West Liao State, 1124-1211).

The Jin armies continued to advance southward, overrunning most of North China. In 1127, they occupied the Song Capital, Bianjing (present day Kaifeng), and took Emperor Song Huizong, the crown prince (later Emperor Song Qinzong), and 3,000 members of the imperial family captive in Wuguocheng, near present day Harbin (Lo, 1956, Vol.1, p.300). This marked the end of the Northern Song Dynasty.

In 1127, Zhao Gou, brother of Emperor Song Qinzong, acceded to the throne as Emperor Song Gaozong (1127-1162) at Nanjing (present day Shangqiu, Henan Province), starting the Southern Song Dynasty (1127-1279). In the face of the Jin attack, he immediately fled to Yangzhou. After the Jin forces crossed the Huai River, he fled again to Hangzhou, and then to Wenzhou. In 1138, he agreed to pay an annual tribute of 250,000 taels of silver and 250,000 bolts of silk to the Jin in exchange for peace. In the same year, he established his capital, which he named Lin'an (meaning Temporary Haven), at Hangzhou. In 1141, he was forced to sign another treaty by which the Southern Song became a subject state to the Jin, paying annual tribute in silver and silk, and to accept the Huai River as the boundary between the two states.

In 1153, the Jin emperor moved his capital from the Harbin area to Youzhoucheng on the site of present day Beijing, and renamed it Zhongdu (Hou, 1980, p.15) (see Figure 9). Soon after he consolidated his power in North China, the Jin emperor started to convert many steppe or mixed marginal areas into arable land, and expanded agriculture on China's northern frontiers. Based on archaeological discoveries, in the twelfth century the Jin government had built several lines of outer fortifications reaching into the steppe, well beyond the traditional Great Wall line, in order to protect its expanded agricultural land and settlements from other northern nomads (Buell, 1979, p.63).

Figure 10   The Distribution of States formed by Nomadic Tribes in the Southern Song Dynasty, 1127-1279.

THE MONGOL EMPIRE OF GENGHIS KHAN, 1227

Genghis Khan (c.1162-1227) was the founder of the Mongol Empire which stretched from the Sea of Japan across Mongolia and Central Asia as far west as the Caspian Sea in 1227. His real name was Temujin and his birth can be placed somewhere between 1150 and 1167 (Hoang, 1990, p.44). His father, Yesugei Khaldun, was the chieftain of the Kiyat, a sub-clan of the Borjigin Mongols. They lived in present day Outer Mongolia, where their economy was based on hunting and herding. They were called the "Black Tatars" by the Nuzhens (Sun, 1951, p.12). This name distinguished them from other Mongol tribes, whom the Nuzhen called the "White Tatars." The White Tatars lived in present day Inner Mongolia, and were both pastoralists and agriculturalist.

According to a Mongolian legend, the Mongols once were united under Kaidu Khan, Kabul Khan and Kutula Khan who were the Khan of all the Mongols (Lister, 1969, p.4). At this time, the title, "khan," meant a "strong man" chosen by his peers to lead a military expedition or a great hunt (Hoang, 1990, p. 104). The Mongols led by their khan lived in the upper reaches of the Onon and Kerulen rivers, which run to the north-east from a massif called the Burkhan Khaldun (now known as the Hentiyn Nuruu). After Kutula Khan's death, the Mongols began fighting among themselves because they did not have a strong chieftain to lead them. Yesugei Khaldun, nephew of Kutula Khan, remained herding in their original homeland on the banks of the Onon and Kerulen rivers. Other Central Asian tribes such as the Tatars (Tantan), Merkits, Naimans, Kereits, and Ongguts raised their flocks elsewhere on grassland on the Mongolian Plateau (Figure 11).

Yesugei Khaldum was killed by the Tatars when his son Temujin was still in his teens. After his death the Kiyat clansmen migrated up the Kerulen river, and settled in the valley of the Burgi, a small tributary running down the slopes of the Burkhan Khaldun. Temujin assumed leadership as he grew up. In 1185, with the help of the Kereits as his ally, he succeeded in subduing the Merkits (Lister, 1969, pp.74-83). Two or three years after this victory, he was elected leader of Kiyat. He continued his efforts to unite other Mongolian tribes and gained the respect of their chieftains. A huraltai, a great assembly of Mongol chieftains which chose a

Figure 11   The Extent of the Mongol Empire of Genghis Khan, 1227.

Khan, was called in 1206 and attended by prominent chieftains such as Prince Altan, Khuchar, Daritai, and Sacha Beki. They could not reach an agreement as to who should be the Khan, but none of them had serious objections to Temujin's leadership. After consulting, they approached Temujin, and made an oath that:

"We appoint you as our Khan. If you will be our Khan, we will go as vanguard against the multitude of your enemies. All the beautiful girls and married women that we capture and all the fine horses, we will give to you. When hunting is afoot, we will be the first to go to the battle and will give you the wild beasts that we surround and catch. If in time of battle we disobey your orders or in time of peace we act contrary to your interests, part us from our wives and possessions and cast us out into the wilderness." (Waley, 1963, p.245)

Temujin accepted the appointment, but he could not be called the Khan of the Mongols because he was not even Khan of a great majority of them. Since the Mongolian chieftains had been receiving titles and official ranks from their Chinese overlords, they decided to choose the Chinese word, Ching or Jeng, (meaning correct, or chief) and added to it the '-s' which the Mongol language demanded (Lister, 1969, p.100). Temujin was thus given the title Chinggis Khan (the "true or chief ruler" or the "universal ruler").

Therefore, Genghis Khan should be correctly spelled and pronounced "Chinggis Khan" (a variant also written Jenghiz Khan). Another explanation of the meaning of Genghis Khan is that the word "genghis" may be Turkic, a variant form of the Tibeto-Mongolian *dalai lama* (meaning, oceanic lama); hence the term, Genghis Khan meant "oceanic khan," i.e. "ruler vast as the ocean," or "universal ruler" (Hoang, 1990, pp. 103-6). Ever since Temujin was designated Genghis Khan (or Chinggis Khan), he has been recorded by posterity under this title.

In the beginning, Genghis Khan commanded only a small number of Mongols in the area of the Onon and Kerulen rivers. After he organized his followers into an effective army, his forces started to subdue one tribe after another on the Mongolia Plateau. He made an alliance with the Jin Emperor in China, and continued to eliminate his rivals on the Mongolian Plateau. The Onggut tribes ("the White Tatars"), living north of the loop of the Huanghe, had long maintained a good relationship with Genghis Khan. The Tenduc Onggut prince sent him a gift of sables and squirrels, and in 1204 even helped him to subdue the Naiman Mongols. Hence, Genghis Khan decreed that the sons of the Onggut princes of Tenduc would be married into the Mongol court and become the imperial sons-in-law (Kessler, 1993, p.156). These conjugal relations started a long series of dynastic alliances between the Onggut princes and the Mongol ruling house (Buel, 1979, p.67).

After he consolidated his power in Mongolia, Genghis Khan started his conquests of other states. He subdued Huigu (the state of the Uygurs), and 1209 invaded Xixia (the state of Dangxiang), forcing the Xixia king to recognize his overlordship. In 1211, Genghis Khan launched the first campaign against Jin (the state of the Sheng Nuzhen). Four years later he entered and destroyed Yanjing, Jin's capital, and compelled the Jin king to acknowledge his overlordship. Then Genghis Khan directed his forces to the west and annexed Xiliao (the state of the Black Qidan). In 1220, he invaded the Empire of Khwarezm (the state of Turco-Iranians), and forced their Emperor Mohammed Shah to flee to Persia. After this victory, Genghis Khan led his forces to invade Xixia again, in reprisal for the refusal of its king to fulfil his treaty obligation to assist him in attacking the Empire of Khwarezm. During the campaign against Xixia, Genghis Khan fell from his horse and died in 1227. One version of the cause of his death was that he was struck by lightning, whilst another is that he drank a poisoned beverage served to him by a concubine (Hoang, 1990, p.19). The exact cause of his death remains a mystery, as does its location. According to the History of the Yuan, he died on the extreme upper reaches of the Xia River (now called the Qing Shui River in Ningxia Hui Autonomous Region) (Martin, 1971, p.302). After his death, a thousand warriors of his Imperial Guard took his body back to his homeland in the Burkhan Khaldun where he was to be buried. In order to keep the funeral procession a secret, the warriors killed everyone they encountered. At the burial site, Genghis Khan's servants were buried with him in order to keep the sepulchre a secret, and the Imperial Guards who had accompanied the funeral caravan were executed as well. [Between 1990 and 1992, a Japanese team tried to locate Genghis Khan's sepulchre without success. However, Maury Kravitz, an Illinois commodities trader, claiming that he had found a crucial reference to the burial site, obtained exclusive rights from the Mongolian government to look for the tomb for five years (Lemonick, 1994, p.68)].

After the death of Genghis Khan, his son, Ogodai (1228-1241), completed the conquest of the Xixia state. He formed an alliance with the Southern Song and launched an attack against the Jin state in 1232, conquering it two years later. In 1235, Ogodai established the capital, Karakorum (Helin in Chinese), in the valley of the Orkhon River, and oversaw the vast Mongol Empire which had been apportioned among his brothers and their descendents, according to the wishes of his father (Martin, 1971, p.309). In the same year, he launched the first invasion of the Southern Song and inflicted heavy losses on the Song forces.

In 1240, a year before his death, Ogodai summoned other Mongol leaders to a council and commanded that an account should be written down of the conquests made by his father and by himself. Hence, the book, *Mangqol'un Niuca Tobca'an* (The Secret History of the Mongols) was written, probably in ancient Uygur script (Lister, 1969, p.x). The book was later transcribed into Chinese characters, probably during the Ming Dynasty, and included in the *Yungle Dadian*, an encyclopedia compiled between 1403 and 1408 (Hung, 1951, p.433). *The Secret History of the Mongols* is one of the very few primary sources of the life history of Genghis Khan, although it was considered by a scholar to be a 'pseudo-historical novel,' because it was difficult to prove, or disprove, the facts related in it (Hoang, 1990, p.16).

Genghis Khan was undoubtedly one of the most brilliant empire builders the world has been. His success was due to his ability to use men of talent, liberal attitudes towards people of different religions, his military strategy, his decisive and ruthless character, and other factors. He knew how to make use of the weather and topography to his advantage. For example, he chose the end of spring when the horses were weak and lean to make a surprise attack on the Naimans, and launched a distant campaign against the Russians during the winter, when the rivers were frozen and his cavalry could move quickly across both

land and water (Jagchid, 1963, p.60). In addition to his military campaigns, Genghis Khan also promoted the Mongol culture. In the early 1200s, he employed two Uygur scholars to develop the Mongolian language in the ancient Uygur script, which was phonetic and quite easily adapted to the Mongolian language (Jagchid and Hyer, 1979, p.210; and Cai et al., 1993, pp. 8-9).

To many Russians and other Europeans he is still considered a brutal and savage conqueror, and the "source of Yellow Peril." However, to the Mongols, he is revered as the ancestor of Mongolian khans and Chinese emperors in the Yuan Dynasty. In 1954, the Chinese government built the Mausoleum of Genghis Khan at Ejin Horo Qi, southeast of Dongsheng on the Ordos Plateau (see Figure 19). This elaborate structure, housing the supposed sarcophagi of Genghis Khan, his wife, and brothers, was built to commemorate him (Kou, 1994, p.26). In 1962 the Chinese government put on an elaborate display of their respect for the celebration of the 800th anniversary of the birth of Genghis Khan, and the Mongolians came from far and wide to Ejin Horo Qi to participate in the celebration. In contrast, in the same year a malignant attack on Genghis Khan and the celebration of his birth appeared first in the Soviet press, and was soon followed by the purge of Tomor-Ochir who organized the celebration in the People's Republic of

Mongolia (Ross, 1978, p.11). However, by the early 1990s, Genghis Khan had been rehabilitated by the government of the People's Republic of Mongolia. In February 1992, the country was renamed the State of Mongolia after it adopted a new constitution which repudiated the socialist system and established a parliamentary government with an elected president. Since then Genghis Khan has been venerated as a national hero, and an icon of Mongolian nationalism by the Mongols in China and Mongolia.

Plate 11
This Boulder Marks the Site of the Legendary Birthplace of Genghis Khan, Near the Town of Dadal, About 300 km Northeast of Ulaan Baatar

THE ESTABLISHMENT OF THE YUAN DYNASTY BY KHUBILAI KHAN, 1271-1368

The Tibetan Empire disintegrated into petty states after 820 mainly due to the confrontation between the Lama Buddhists and the traditional Bon followers, and the rivalry between different sects of Lamaism (Carrasco, 1959, p.19). Making use of this situation of disunity, Prince Godan, the second son of Ogodai, invaded Tibet in 1240 (Shakabpa, 1967, p.61). After the conquest, Prince Godan appointed Sakya Pandita, the Lama of the Sakyapa (or Flower Sect), to be his "Vice-Regent" to rule Tibet (Shakabpa, 1967, p.63 and Walt van Praag, 1987, p.5). The Lama introduced Lama Buddhism and Tibetan culture to Prince Godan, and established a priest-patron relationship. Because of this close relationship, Lama Buddhism began to diffuse throughout the Mongol Empire.

Khubilai (1259-1294) succeeded his brother, Mongke, and proclaimed himself the Great Khan in 1260. In the same year, Khubilai transferred his capital from Karakorum to Shangdu (meaning Upper Capital) near the present site of Zhenglan Banner (Figure 12). In order to facilitate his control of China, in 1262 he started to build a new capital, Dadu (the Great Capital) on the present site of Beijing (see Figure 9). Dadu (also known as Khanbalik or called Cambaluc by Marco Polo) was completed in 1266. Khubilai then used it regularly as a winter capital. Shangdu remained as the summer capital (Worden and Savada, 1991, p.23).

In 1271, Khubilai Khan proclaimed himself the emperor of a new state, which he called Dayuan (Great Yuan), and instructed his general Bayan to lead a Mongol force of 200,000 to invade the Southern Song (Bai, 1982, p.292). In 1276, Bayan reached Lin'an, the capital of the Southern Song, and captured Emperor Song Gongdi and the two empresses. This virtually ended the Southern Song Dynasty. In the same year, Khubilai Khan shifted his political centre into China by moving his capital from Shangdu to Dadu, and completing the conquest of the Southern Song in 1279.

Khubilai Khan was the first Mongol khan to rule the entire territory of the Han people. He became Emperor Yuan Shizu of the Yuan Dynasty (1271-1368), and gave his grandfather the posthumous title of Emperor Yuan Taizu. He made Mongolia part of his Chinese Empire, and considered himself as the Great Khan of the Mongols and the Emperor of the Chinese.

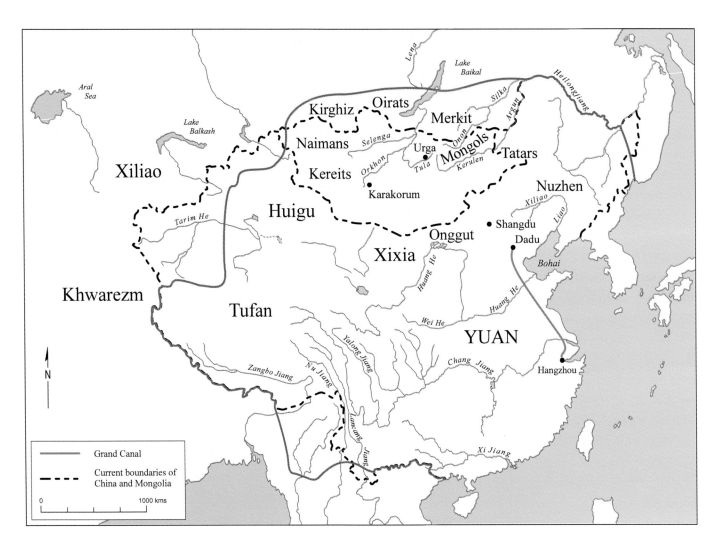

Figure 12 The Yuan Empire of Khubilai Khan, 1271-1368.

Unlike other Mongolian chiefs, Khubilai Khan recognized the economic and political importance of agriculture. Soon after his conquest of Song, he pacified the Han people and promoted agriculture. In peace time, he ordered soldiers to carry out various water conservation projects, such as reclaiming land and developing arable farming. He extended the Grand Canal from Hangzhou to Dadu, and improved the transportation of commodities between Central China and North China.

Khubilai Khan was still a Mongol at heart, although he was an Emperor of the Han people. The imperial family and the related nobility remained purely Mongolian in language, customs and culture (Schurmann, 1956, p.306). They made no attempt to become a part of the Han gentry, nor did they try to usurp their property rights. The Mongols followed many socio-economic practices of the Han people but they did not lose their identify. They had considerable impact on Han culture and science because of their extensive contacts with various ethnic groups in Central Asia and Eastern Europe. Partly through the Mongol nomads, for example, European technology such as the manufacture of cloisonné was introduced to China, while Chinese innovations such as block printing were diffused to Europe. Because of their close contacts with Tibet, Mongolians acquired the Lamaist therapy which was known to be very effective for trauma surgery and the setting of fractured bones (Ma, 1989, p.67). Other outstanding scientific and cultural contributions of the Mongols to China included veterinary science, astronomy, mathematics, music, dance, horsemanship, and archery.

Of the European visitors to China during the Yuan Dynasty, Marco Polo, a Venetian merchant from Italy, was by far the best known traveller. In 1271, accompanied by his father and uncle, he crossed Central Asia by camel, arriving at Shangdu four years later. Here they were welcomed by Khubilai Khan. During his 17 years in China, Marco Polo visited many places in the Yuan Empire, and was entrusted by Khubilai Khan with several administrative jobs. After he returned to his home in Venice, he wrote a book, *Travels of Marco Polo*, which described the prosperous empire of the Khubilai Khan. It was so widely read in Europe that some historians believe that it might have inspired Christopher Columbus and other European explorers to look for a route to Asia.

Although Lamaist Buddhism was the most dominant faith in the Yuan Dynasty, Khubilai Khan and his successors were tolerant towards other religions. Hence, Daoism, Confucianism, Christianity and Islam also flourished during the Yuan Dynasty. One of the most important roles of the Tibetan lamas was the introduction of a new Mongolian writing, based on the Tibetan script. After he became the Emperor of the Yuan Dynasty, Khubilai Khan issued decrees both in Uygur Mongolian script and in Chinese characters. Soon he found it very awkward to use these scripts together on posters because the Uygur script ran horizontally and the Chinese characters read vertically. Accordingly, he asked the Tibetan Lama Phagspa to create a new form of writing based on the Tibetan script, which ran vertically like the Chinese characters (Lister, 1969, p.xi). Henceforth, the Phagspa script replaced the ancient Uygur script.

Plate 12   *Khubilai Khan*

THE KHALKHAS AND OIRATS IN THE MING DYNASTY, 1368-1644

The Mongolian rule of China lasted only 91 years. The Mongols were then driven back to the Mongolian Plateau by Zhu Yuanzhang who started the Ming Dynasty (1368-1644) of the Han people. He established his capital at Jinling in 1368, which he renamed Nanjing. He adopted the strategy of destroying the unity of the Mongols by playing one tribe off against the others. Partly because of this "divide and rule" policy, the Mongols were broken into two main branches in the fourteenth century: the Khalkhas in eastern Mongolia, and the Oirats in western Mongolia (Figure 13). Since 1400, these two branches had been fighting against each other. These conflicts lasted for more than 50 years (Worden and Savada, 1991, p.31). In 1410, making use of their civil war, Emperor Yong Le (1403-1424) mobilized over 100,000 men to invade Mongolia, and subdued both the Khalkhas and the Oirats (Sun, 1951, p.22). He decided then to establish a new capital in North China in order to strengthen the defence of the northern frontiers. In 1404, he started to build a new capital called Beijing on the site of Dadu (see Figure 9). The new city took about 16 years to complete. It consisted of Outer City and Inner City; the latter enclosed an Imperial City which in turn enclosed the Forbidden City. In 1420, Emperor Yong Le moved the Ming capital from Nanjing to Beijing.

By the middle of the fifteenth century the Oirats, under the leadership of Esen Khan, had succeeded in defeating the Khalkhas and uniting much of Mongolia. In 1449, they invaded China, ransacked Datong, and took Emperor Ming Yingzong (1436-1449) as a prisoner (Sun, 1954, p.23-24). However, soon after Esen Khan was killed in the battle, the leaderless Oirats were defeated by the Ming forces, and driven back to Mongolia. They were forced to return to Emperor Ming Yingzong to China in 1450, and resumed their tribute relationship with the Ming.

The Mongols were disunited again. The Oirats controlled western Mongolia and part of the present day Xinjiang Uygur Autonomous Region. The Khalkhas occupied the grasslands north and south of the Gobi Desert. The Ordos Mongols and the Chahar Mongols formed a loose confederation in present day Inner Mongolia. Although they were constantly fighting with each other, they shared a continuing hostility

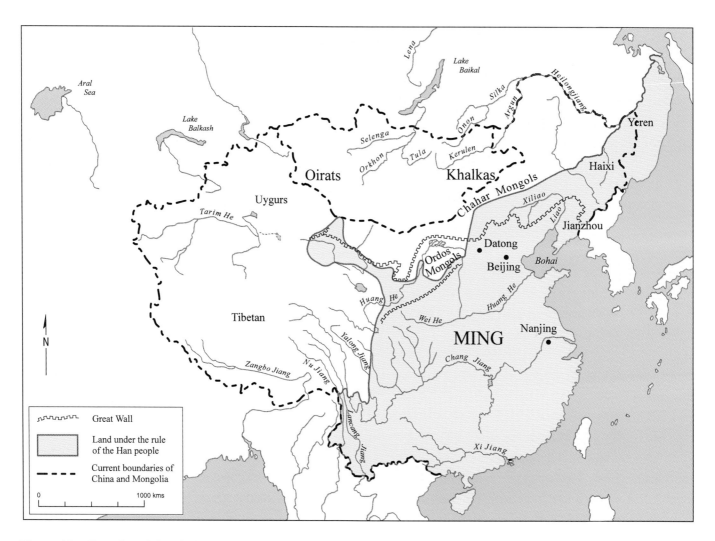

Figure 13   Location of the Khalkhas and Oirats in the Ming Dynasty, 1368-1644.

to the Chinese. The Khalkhas, led by their leader Altan Khan (1507-1583), rose to power again, and invaded China again in 1550, plundering the areas around Beijing before withdrawing (Sun, 1951, p.25). Then Altan Khan turned his attention to other Mongol tribes. In 1552 he defeated the Oirats and united most of Mongolia again. Throughout the early sixteenth century he expanded his territory in present day Qinghai Province and the Xinjiang Ugyur Autonomous Region. He supported the Gelugpa (Yellow Sect) militarily against other sects in Tufan (Tibet), and built a strong alliance in 1578 with the Tufan by conferring the title of Dalai Lama upon Sonam Gyatso (1543-1588), the abbot of Drepung Monastery, and the most eminent lama of the Yellow Sect (Shakabpa, 1967, p.95; Wang and Suo, 1984, p.87). "La" in Tibetan language means "superior" and "ma" means "none" (Sinha, 1964, pp. 17-18). So "Lama" means "without superior," or "the one who has no superior," or "the supreme master." "Dalai" means "ocean." Hence Dalai Lama means the "supreme master with knowledge as wide and deep as an ocean." This priest-patron relationship benefited both Altan Khan and the Yellow Sect: it gave Altan Khan legitimacy and religious sanction for his imperial pretensions, and it helped the Yellow sect achieve a pre-eminent position in Tibetan Buddhism (Warden and Savada, 1991, p.100). Altan Khan was responsible for reintroducing Tibetan Buddhism to the Mongol society (Embree, 1988, Vol. 3, p.314).

Sonam Gyatso was said to be the third reincarnation of the two previous lamas, as the incarnate lama system developed during the sixteenth century. After his death, his reincarnation was said to be Altan Khan's great-grandson, and both the fourth and fifth Dalai Lamas claimed to be reincarnations of Mongols (Snellgrove and Richardson, 1968, p.184). By the early seventeenth century, most of the Khalkhas had been converted to Lama Buddhism, which then became the state religion of Mongolia.

Although he succeeded in subduing other Mongol tribes and the Tufan, Altan Khan realized that he could not conquer China. In 1570, he signed a peace treaty with Emperor Ming Muzong (1567-1572), and accepted the title of Shunyi Wang (King of Obedience and Righteousness) (Sun, 1951, p.25). As Altan Khan became a devoted Buddhist, he maintained a peaceful relationship with China. On the other hand the Ming emperors also encouraged the introduction of Lama Buddhism to the warlike Mongols in the hope that they would lead a peaceful nomadic life on the grassland. Therefore, in 1587, soon after Sonam Gyatso acquired the title of Dalai Lama, Emperor Ming Shenzong (1573-1619) recognized this title and let the new Dalai Lama rule the Tufan.

Although they constantly felt the threat of the Mongol invasion, the Ming emperors had no problems with the nomadic tribes in north-eastern China. In the early sixteenth century three groups of Nuzhen tribes in north-eastern China could be identified: the Jianzhou Nuzhen in the eastern part of the Liao River; the Haixi Nuzhen in the middle and lower reaches of the Songhua River; and the Yeren Nuzhen at the confluence of the Heilongjiang and Songhua River (Lo, 1956, Vol. 2, pp. 26-7). They posed no threat to China since they were not militarily strong and therefore submitted to Ming rule.

Plate13 *A Khalkha Horseman*

THE INNER AND OUTER MONGOLIA DURING THE QING DYNASTY, 1644-1911

According to a Manchu legend, Fokulun, a beautiful fairy, was bathing near Buir Lake and immaculately conceived after eating the fruit given to her by a magpie. Then she gave birth to a son who became the ancestor of the Aisin Gioro clan (Yim, 1994, p.109). In 1593, Nurhachi of the clan (1559-1626) was elected chief of the Jianzhou Nuzhen. After he had subdued other tribes in north-eastern China in 1616, he declared himself Great Khan and established the Great Jin state (the Later Jin), as though to continue the Jin State of 1115-1234 (Sun, 1951, p.26). Two years later, he launched the first attack against the Ming, and moved his capital from Liaoyang to Shengjing (present day Shenyang). After his death, his son, Huangtaiji, subdued the nomadic tribes in Inner Mongolia, and continued to expand his territory at the expense of the Ming. In 1636, Huangtaiji changed the name of his state to the Great Qing, and the name of Jianzhou Nuzhen to Manchu, declaring himself the Manchu Emperor of the Great Qing. Fulin, his third son, succeeded him after his death in 1643, and toppled the Ming Dynasty. In 1644, Fulin assumed the title of Emperor Shunzhi (1644-1661), the first emperor of the Qing Dynasty (1644-1911). He saw the advantage of recognizing the authority of the Dalai Lama also and of using his influence to deter the Mongol tribes from invading his empire in China (Xie, 1935, pp.23-26). Accordingly, in 1652 he conferred upon the fifth Dalai Lama a special title, "the Great, Righteous and Complacent Buddha of the Western Heaven Dalai Lama," and recognized his religious power over the Mongols. Since that date the Yellow Sect, led by the Dalai Lama, has been the dominant sect and major political force in Tibet. The term "Tibet" was first used in 1663, during the reign the second Manchu Emperor Kangxi (1662-1722).

While the Manchu were fully occupied in consolidating their power in Tibet and China, the Mongolian tribes were at war with each other. The Oirats, led by Galdan (1676-1697), invaded eastern Mongolia in 1688 and drove the Khalkhas southward into Inner Mongolia. In response to the Khalkhas' appeal for help, the Manchu sent troops to fight against the Oirats, drove them back to the west in 1696, and helped the Khalkhas to resettle in Mongolia. Mongolia was then divided into Outer Mongolia and Inner Mongolia; this

Figure 14   Inner and Outer Mongolia in the Qing Dynasty, 1670.

marked the beginning of the terms "Inner" and "Outer" Mongolia (Figure 14). The Khalkha princes were permitted to run Outer Mongolia and became vassals of the Manchu emperor. Inner Mongolia, which was placed directly under Manchu rule, was divided into seven *meng* (or leagues, comparable to prefectures), each of which was subdivided into a number of *qi* (or banners, comparable to counties), and run by the Manchu Ambans (Manchu high-ranking officials residing in Inner Mongolia) (Embree, 1988, Vol. 3, p.325).

The Anglo-French threat to invade China again gave the Russians a chance to advance their East Asia interests. In return for her mediation of the dispute between China and Britain and France, the Manchu ceded to Russia all land north of the Heilongjiang by the Treaty of Aigun, 1858, and all land east of the Ussuri and east of Lake Balkash by the Treaty of Peking, 1860. After the Russo-Japanese War of 1904-1905, fought in Manchuria, the Manchu government started to sponsor emigration of Chinese to both Manchuria and Mongolia in an effort to prevent their sparsely populated vast lands from being occupied by the Russians or Japanese (Yakhontoff, 1936, p.14). Many areas in the eastern and southern borders of Inner Mongolia were incorporated into provinces of Manchuria and other Chinese border provinces. Towards the end of the Qing Dynasty the Han people had overtaken the Mongols as the largest ethnic group in Inner Mongolia.

Plate 14 *A Kazakh Woman Milking a Cow*

51

THE EMERGENCE OF THE MONGOLIAN PEOPLE'S REPUBLIC, 1924-1946

The Xing Zhong Hui (The Reviving China Society) was formed by Dr. Sun Yat-sen (1866-1925) in 1894 with the objective of overthrowing the Manchu, expelling the "barbarians," and establishing a republican government for the Han people. Traditionally, both the Mongolians and the Manchu were suspicious of the Han Chinese who considered them "barbarians." The Mongols only swore allegiance to the Manchu emperor or the Mongolian khan but they would not accept the sovereignty of a new republic under the Han. Soon after the Wuchang Uprising on 10 October 1911 and the declaration of the Republic of China, the Khalkha princes in Outer Mongolia did not want to be ruled by the Han people and therefore declared independence. The eighth Jebtsundamba Khutukhtu, the Living Buddha of Urga, was proclaimed the head of the newly created Mongolian state and took the title of Bogdo-Gegen (the Holy Emperor). Meanwhile, after the downfall of the Manchu, the Mongolians in Inner Mongolia looked to Outer Mongolia and Japan for support. However, Yuan Shih-k'ai, the President of the Republic of China, promoted in rank and title all Mongol nobles who supported him, and appointed most of the Mongolian leaders in Beijing to positions of officers in his special guards (Jagchid, 1979, pp. 107-8). Thus he succeeded in checking the independence movement in Inner Mongolia.

The Russian Tsar had always tried to extend his influence in Outer Mongolia and Manchuria. Although he supported the attempt of the Khalkhas in Outer Mongolia to break away from China, he did not want to assist them to unite with Inner Mongolia and create a strong Mongolian state. Hence the Tsar agreed with China in November 1913 that China would continue to rule Inner Mongolia, but recognize the autonomy of Outer Mongolia. In June 1915 the Tripartite Treaty of Kyakhta was signed by tsarist Russia, China, and Outer Mongolia, defining the boundary between Outer and Inner Mongolia, and recognizing Chinese overlordship of an autonomous Outer Mongolia.

After the Russian Bolshevik Revolution in 1917 the White Russian forces took refuge in Outer Mongolia and in February 1921 occupied Urga (Kulun in Chinese). In the following month the Mongolian revolutionaries living in Russia organized the Mongolian People's Party and appealed to the Soviets for help.

The Red Army troops responded quickly by entering Outer Mongolia, taking Urga in July 1921, driving out the White Russians and installing the Mongolian People's Party in the capital. As a consequence, Outer Mongolia became a virtual protectorate of the U.S.S.R. After the death in July 1924 of the eighth Jebtsundamba Khutukhtu, the Living Buddha of Urga, no new incarnation was permitted. Outer Mongolia took the official name of the Mongolian People's Republic in August, and Urga was renamed Ulaan Baatar (meaning Red Hero). A new sense of national pride was growing among the Soviet-educated intelligentsia while the Mongolian people in general were being indoctrinated with Russian communism and integrated into Russian culture.

To prevent the expansion of the Russian influence beyond the Gobi Desert, China divided Inner Mongolia into four provinces in 1928 (Figure 15). Each of these provinces, namely, Ninghsia (Ningxia), Suiyuan, Chahar (Chahaer), and Jehol (Rehe), consisted partly of Inner Mongolian territory and partly of China's provinces of Gansu, Shaanxi, Shanxi, Hebei, and Liaoning. As a result of these administrative changes and the increasing in-migration of the Han people, the Han people outnumbered the Mongolians by a ratio of four to one in the four new provinces, reducing them to the status of a national minority in their original homeland (Dufour, 1973, p.65)

On 7 July 1937, Japan invaded China. Having occupied part of Inner Mongolia in 1938, the Japanese formed the Federative Autonomous Government of Inner Mongolia in 1938. This puppet government ceased to exist soon after the Japanese surrendered on 14 August 1945. On the same day the U.S.S.R. and China signed the Treaty of Friendship and Alliance, by which the Chinese government agreed to hold a plebiscite in Outer Mongolia on the issue of independence. This plebiscite, held on 20 October 1945, showed an almost unanimous vote in favour of independence. Accordingly, on 5 January 1946 China recognized Outer Mongolia as an independent republic. China agreed to exchange diplomatic representatives but this did not occur, partly because of the civil war between the Nationalists and the Communists.

Figure 15   The Reorganization of Inner Mongolia, 1928.

THE ESTABLISHMENT OF INNER MONGOLIAN AUTONOMOUS REGION, 1947

In November 1945, the Chinese Community Party assisted the Communist Mongols in Inner Mongolia to set up an organization at Zhangjiakou (Kalgan) to carry out their autonomy movement (Wang, 1957, p.10). Soon after the Nationalists were driven out, an Inner Mongolian Autonomous Region (*Nei Mongol Zizhiqu*) was established, on 1 May 1947, and Zhangjiakou was made the capital. Ulanfu, formerly head of the Nationalities Academy responsible for training cadres from among national minorities in Yenan, became chairman of the region (Heaton, 1978, p.64). [Ulanfu remained leader of Inner Mongolia for 20 years until he was purged during the Cultural Revolution (1966-69). He was accused of being a pan-Mongol nationalist, dreaming of becoming a modern Genghis Khan and establishing an independent Mongol kingdom (Heaton, 1978, p.65). In April 1967 he was dismissed from all his positions, including commander of the Inner Mongolian Military Region and First Secretary of the Chinese Community Party (Hyer and Heaton, 1968, p.123)].

After the People's Republic of China was established on 1 October 1949, the new government clearly stated its policies toward national minorities. One of these policies was that any minority people living in a compact community that was large enough to form an administrative unit would be permitted to establish an autonomous area with its own organs of self-government. Based on population size, autonomous areas were classified into three levels: autonomous regions, *meng* (or leagues, comparable to prefectures), and *qi* (or banners, comparable to counties). The Mongolians, for example, have their autonomous region equivalent to a province. In addition, Mongolian autonomous prefectures and banners were established in other provinces where Mongols lived in compact communities. These included two Mongolian autonomous prefectures of Boertala and Bayinguoleng in the Xinjiang Uygur Autonomous Region, the Mongolian and Kazakh Autonomous Prefecture in Qinghai Province, and seven autonomous banners in the provinces of Liaoning, Jilin, Heilongjiang, Gansu, and Qinghai, and Xinjiang Uygur Autonomous Region (Ma, 1989, p.64).

According to the 1990 census, China's Mongol population totaled 4,806,849, making them the eighth largest ethnic minority, though they accounted for only 0.42 percent of China's total population (Table 4).

About 70 percent of these Mongols lived in Inner Mongolian Autonomous Region, 12 percent in Liaoning, and the remaining 18 percent in other parts of China (Table 5). However, the Autonomous Region was predominately peopled by the Han, who accounted for about 80 percent of the region's total population, whereas Mongols constituted only 16 percent (Table 6). The remaining 4 percent belonged to over 48 other ethnic minorities.

The boundary of the Inner Mongolian Autonomous Region has been changed several times since 1947. In that year it included only the northern half of its present area (Figure 16). Throughout the 1950s the Chinese government had been expanding the territory of Inner Mongolia to include the areas where Mongols lived in compact communities. The province of Chahar (Chahaer) was abolished in 1952 and merged with Shanxi, Hebei, and Inner Mongolian Autonomous Region (Jiang, 1994, p.2). In March 1954, the province of Suiyuan was abolished and became part of Inner Mongolia. In April 1954 the city of Kueisui was renamed Hohhot and made the capital of the autonomous region (Gao, 1955, p.22). Two years later the province of Jehol (Rehe) was abolished and merged with Inner Mongolia, Hebei, and Liaoning. In 1957 Inner Mongolia was enlarged further to include parts of Ninghsia (Ningxia) and Gansu provinces. In the following year, the Ningxia Hui Autonomous Region was established (Figure 17).

Table 4   Ethnic Composition of China's Population, 1990

Ethnic Group	Number of Persons (in thousands)	Percentage
Han	1,042,482	91.96
Zhuang	15,490	1.37
Manchu	9,821	0.87
Hui	8,603	0.76
Miao	7,398	0.65
Uygur	7,214	0.64
Yi	6,572	0.58
Tujia	5,704	0.50
Mongol	4,807	0.42
Tibetan	4,593	0.41
Buyi	2,545	0.22
Dong	2,514	0.22
Yao	2,134	0.19
Korean	1,921	0.17
Bai	1,595	0.14
Hani	1,254	0.11
Kazakh	1,112	0.10
Li	1,111	0.10
Dai	1,025	0.09
She	630	0.06
Lisu	575	0.05
Others*	4,583	0.40
Total	**1,133,683**	**100.00**

* These included 35 other ethnic groups, many unidentified ethnic groups, and 3,421 foreigners who had Chinese citizenship.

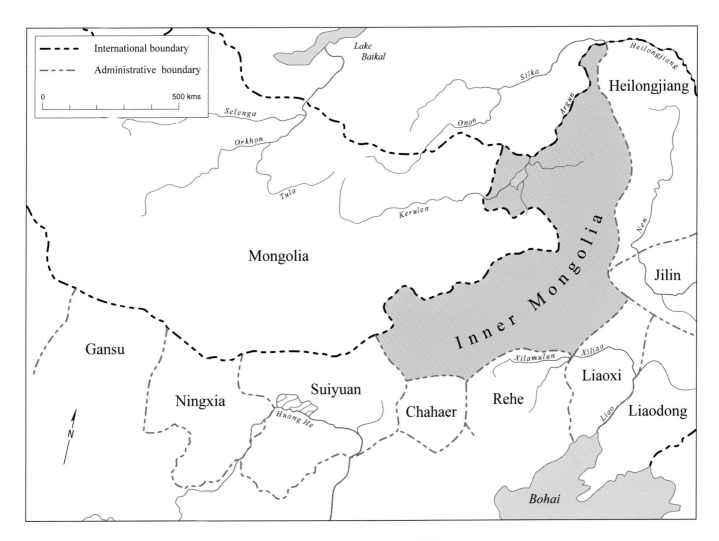

Figure 16   The Boundary of the Inner Mongolian Autonomous Region, 1953.

Table 5   Distribution of Mongols in China, 1990

Location	No. of Persons	Percentage
Inner Mongolia	3,379,738	70.4
Liaoning	587,311	12.2
Jilin	156,488	3.3
Hebei	141,833	3.0
Heilongjiang	139,077	2.9
Xinjiang	138,021	2.8
Qinghai	71,510	1.5
Henan	66,015	1.4
Sichuan	27,303	0.6
Beijing	16,833	0.4
Hubei	5,632	0.1
Others	72,646	1.5
Total	**4,802,407**	**100.00**

In March 1969 border clashes between China and Russia broke out at Zhenbao (Damansky) Island in the Wusuli Jiang (Ussuri River), and in July at another island in the Heilongjiang (Amur River). The Chinese government decided to reduce the area of Inner Mongolia in order to improve its military capacity to fight against the Soviet Union and the People's Republic of Mongolia (renamed the State of Mongolia in 1992), and to diminish the political problem posed by its Mongol minority along the Sino-Mongolian and Sino-Russian borders (Figure 18). Two eastern mengs were transferred to the provinces of Heilongjiang and Liaoning, and several western qi were absorbed by Ningxia

Hui Autonomous Region and Gansu Province. The Sino-Russian relationship improved in the late 60s, and the Chinese Government changed the boundary of Inner Mongolia back to its 1968 boundary after 1981.

Today the autonomous region is divided administratively into eight prefectures, and four regional cities (Hohhot, Baotao, Chifeng, and Wuhai) which are directly under the administration of the government of the autonomous region (Figure 19). The prefectures and regional cities administer a total of 54 banners which include Oroqen, Ewenkizu and Daurzu Autonomous Banners, 18 counties, 12 county-level cities, and 16 city-administered districts (Jiang, 1994, p.4).

Table 6   Ethnic Composition of Inner Mongolia, 1990

Ethnic Group	No. of Persons	Percentage
Han	17,289,995	80.58
Mongol	3,379,738	15.78
Manchu	460,517	2.15
Hui	192,725	0.90
Daur	71,484	0.33
Ewenki	23,379	0.11
Korean	22,173	0.10
Russian	4,388	0.02
Oroqen	3,110	0.02
Xibe	2,867	0.01
Zhuang	1,503	0.01
Miao	848	0.00
Others	3,791	0.02
TOTAL	**21,456,518**	**100.00**

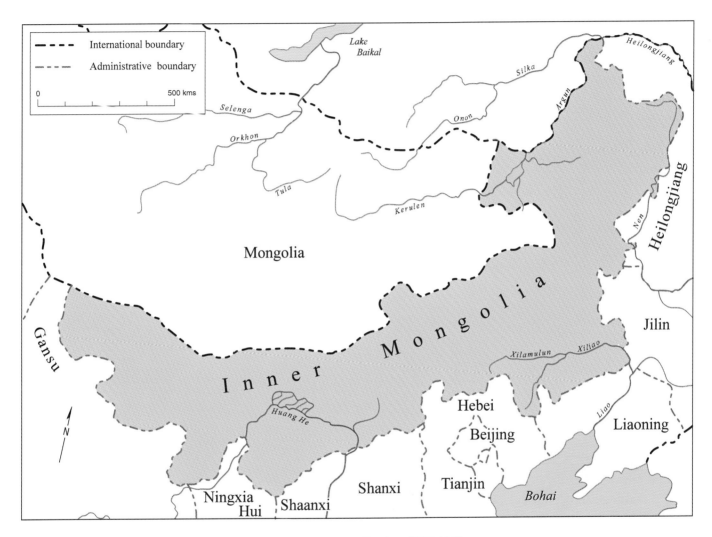

Figure 17   The Boundary of the Inner Mongolian Autonomous Region, 1957-1968.

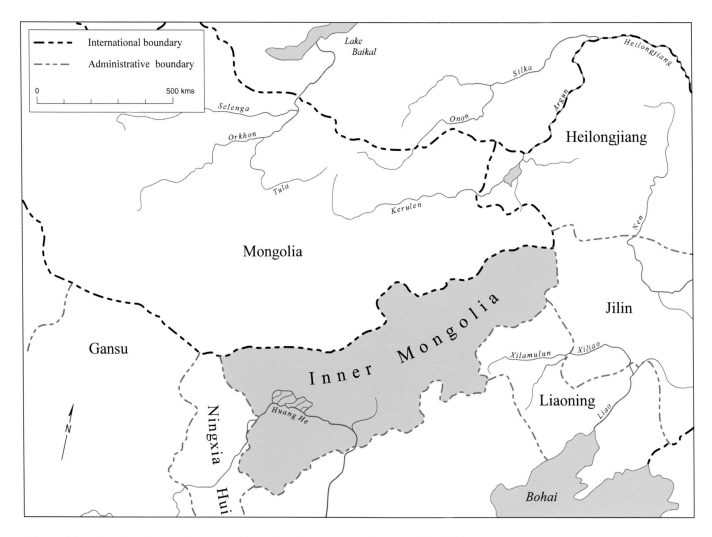

Figure 18 The Boundary of the Inner Mongolian Autonomous Region, 1969-1978.

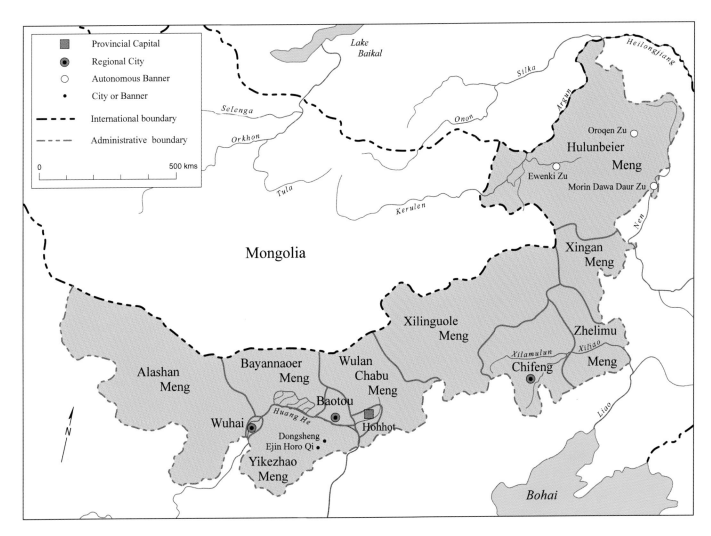

Figure 19 Political Divisions of the Inner Mongolian Autonomous Region, 1994.

EPILOGUE

The history and geography of the Mongols have been studied and researched more than those of other Eurasian nomads, partly because of their Mongol Empire in the thirteenth century, and partly because of their strategic location in Central Asia at the beginning of the twentieth century as a buffer zone between the contending powers of Russia, Japan, and China (Lattimore, 1951, pp.28-40; Hung, 1951, pp.433-492). The relationship between the non-Han nomads and Han agriculturalists in China's northern frontiers seems to be a history of war and peace. The occupation of the Chinese territory by the northern tribes was sporadic, depending on their strength relative to that of the Han people. If the northern tribes were united under a strong leader, they would invade China, especially when China had a weak central government. At various times they succeeded in conquering China partially or entirely, and ruled the Han people under their dynasties. For example, North China was occupied by the Tuoba Xianbei, who established the Northern Wei (A.D. 386-534); by the Qidan, who established the Liao (907-1125), and by the Sheng Nuzhen, who established the Jin (1115-1234). The entire territory of China was controlled by the Mongols, who established the Yuan Dynasty (1271-1368), and by the Manchu who established the Qing Dynasty (1644-1911). However, when the Han people had a strong central government, their emperors sent military expeditions to subdue the northern tribes, and used the policy of "divide and rule" to reduce their threat, encouraging one tribe to fight with another, and preventing them from forming a strong confederation. The Han people also formed military alliances with one nomadic tribe to subdue another nomadic group, or overthrow their own rivals in China. For example, the Uygurs assisted the Tang emperor to fight against the Qiang (Tibetans) whereas the Qidan helped Shi Jingtang to establish the late Tang Dynasty in North China. In addition to the use of military force, the Chinese emperors also tried other means to pacify the nomadic chieftains, such as awarding titles to them, sending them gifts, and establishing relationship with them through marriage (Lattimore, 1936, p.391). China's frontiers would be secure as long as the chieftains had vested interests which they did not want to lose in wars. It was also the policy of the Chinese emperors not to control the non-Han tribes, but to integrate them into the Han society; a high level of integration prevented invasion and increased loyalty to the emperor.

Nation-states have risen and fallen on the Mongolian Plateau and in China's northern frontiers throughout the four thousand years of Chinese history. Archaeological excavations in Inner Mongolia reveal that, in addition to the warfare in China's northern frontier, there had also been many economic and cultural exchanges between the nomadic states and the Chinese empires. For example, in the spring of 1980, remnants of ivory *suanchou* were found at an ancient Qidan tomb in Hudongba Village (Anon, 1984, p.31). *Suanchou* were calculating instruments first used during the Zhou Dynasty in c.1000 B.C. until they were replaced by the abacus during the Ming Dynasty (A.D. 1368-1644). This discovery shows that, as early as the tenth century B.C., ancient mathematics and calculating instruments had been diffused from the Han people to the northern tribes. In fact, most of the non-Han emperors had been sinicized to a certain degree before they established their dynasties in China. In the process of their political control of the Han people, the non-Han rulers adopted the Han system of government and became more assimilated into the Han culture. The non-Han people were always referred to as "barbarians" in the Chinese historical records. In fact, the culture and technology of the northern nomads were not necessarily inferior to those of the Han people. In the past, the non-Han people brought their cultural attributes to China and enriched the development of the Chinese culture. For example, Yuezhi were given the credit for introducing the famous Hetian jade stones and promoting the diffusion of Buddhism to China during the East Han Dynasty (Kessler, 1993, pp.20-21). The Mongols and other nomadic people played an important role in introducing some Middle East musical instruments to China where they were adopted and modified to become today's typical Chinese musical instruments, such as *erhu* (two-stringed violin) and *pipa* (Chinese guitar). The history of China's northern frontiers is, therefore, by no means just a history of conflicts between the Han and non-Han people. It is also a history of economic and cultural exchanges, assimilation and integration of pastoral and agricultural societies, and alliances of the Han and northern peoples.

Plate 15   *Typical Mongolian Camels*

REFERENCES

Anon. "Oldest Math Instrument Found," *Beijing Review*, July 16, 1984, p. 31.

Anon. "The Military Line of Genghis Khan (II)," *Beijing Review*, May 30-June 5, 1994, pp. 26-27.

Atwood, Christopher and Lincoln Kaye. "Two Mongolias 2: The Han Hordes," *Far Eastern Economic Review* 9 April 1992, 18-19.

Bai Shouyi. *An Outline History of China* Beijing: Foreign Languages Press, 1982.

Bawden, C.R. *The Modern History of Mongolia*. London: Kegan Paul International Ltd. 1989.

Brent, Peter. *The Mongol Empire: Genghis Khan*. London: Weidenfeld and Nicolson, 1976.

Buell, Paul D. "The Role of the Sino-Mongolian Frontier Zone in the Rise of Cinggis-Qan," in *Studies on Mongolia: Proceedings of the First North American Conference on Mongolian Studies*, edited by Henry G. Schwarz, Bellingham: Western Washington University, 1979, pp. 63-76

Cai, Zhichun, Hong Yongbin, and Wang Longgeng (Ed.). *Mengguzu Wenhua* (The Mongolian Culture). Beijing: Chinese Social Science Publishes, 1993 (in Chinese script).

Carrasco Pizana, Pedro. *Land and Polity in Tibet*. Seattle: University of Washington Press, 1959.

Cleaves, Francis Woodman. *The Secret History of the Mongols* (Volume 1 - Translation). Cambridge, Mass.: Harvard University Press, 1982

Cressey, George B. "Chinese Colonization in Mongolia: A General Survey," *American Geographical Society Special Publication No. 14: Pioneer Settlement*, New York, 1932, pp. 273-287.

Cressey, George B. "The Ordos Desert of Inner Mongolia," *Denison University Bulletin, Journal of the Scientific Laboratories*, Vol. XXVIII, October 1933, pp 155-248.

Cressey, George B. "The Deserts of Asia," *Journal of Asian Studies*, Vol. XIX, No. 4, August 1960, pp. 389-402.

Deng, Shulin. "Inner Mongolian Autonomous Region," *Zhongguo Jianshe* (China Reconstruct), May 1987, pp. 77-80 (in Chinese script).

Dufour, Charles. "Inner Mongolia as a Case Study of the Question of National Minorities" (translated from French into Chinese), *Qishi Niandai Yuekan* No. 40, 1973, pp. 65-68.

Embree, Ainslie T. (Ed.). *Encyclopedia of Asia History.* New York: Charles Scribner's Sons, 1988, Vol. 1 to Vol. 4.

Fairbank, John K., Edwin O. Reischauer, and Albert M. Craig. *East Asia: Tradition and Transformation.* Boston: Houghton Mifflin Co., 1978.

Friters, Gerard M. *Outer Mongolia and Its International Position* Baltimore: Johns Hopkins Press, 1949.

Gao, Ge. *Weida Zuguo di Nei Mongol Zizhiqu* (The Great Motherland's Inner Mongolian Autonomous Region). Shanghai: New Knowledge Press, 1955. (in Chinese script).

Gernet, Jacques. *A History of Chinese Civilization* (translated by J.R. Foster). Cambridge: Cambridge University Press, 1989.

Grousset, Rene. *Conqueror of the World* (translated by Marian McKellar and Denis Sinor). New York: The Orion, 1966.

Hartog, Leo de. *Genghis Khan: Conqueror of the World.* New York: St. Martin's Press, 1989.

Heaton, William. "Ulanfu: Sketch of a Mongolian Careeer Through Crisis," *The Canada-Mongolia Review*, Vol. IV, No.1, April 1978, pp. 63-69.

Hoang, Michel. *Genghis Khan* (translated by Ingrid Cranfield). New York: New Amsterdam Books, 1990.

Hou, Renzhi. *Lishishang de Beijingcheng* (The History of the City of Beijing). Beijing: Chinese Youth Publisher, 1980 (in Chinese script).

Hung, Willaim. "The Transmission of the Book Known as the Secret History of the Mongols," *Harvard Journal of Asiatic Studies*, Vol. 14, 1951, pp.433-92.

Hyer, Paul and William Heaton. "The Cultural Revolution in Inner Mongolia," *China Quarterly* No. 36, Dec. 1968, pp. 114-128.

Jagchid, Sechin. "The Inner Mongolian Response to the Chinese Republic, 1911-1917," in *Studies on Mongolia: Proceedings of the First North American Conference on Mongolian Studies*, edited by Henry G. Schwarz, Bellingham: Western Washington University, 1979, pp. 102-11.

Jagchid, Sechin and Paul Hyer. *Mongolia's Culture and Society* Boulder, Colorado: Westview Press, 1979.

Jagchid, S. "Genghis Khan's Military Strategy and Art of War" (translated by Albert E. Dien), *Chinese Culture* Vol. 5 No.2 Oct. 1963, pp. 59-62.

Jiang, Changyu. A Letter, dated 26 Oct. 1994, to Dr. David Lai, pp. 1-4 (unpublished Chinese script).

Kaye, Lincoln. "Two Mongolias 1: Faltering Steppes," *Far Eastern Economic Review* 9 April 1992, 16-18.

Kaye, Lincoln. "Two Mongolias 3: Back to the Old Faith," *Far Eastern Economic Review* 9 April 1992, 20.

Kessler, Adam T. *Empire Beyond the Great Wall: the Heritage of Genghis Khan.* Los Angeles: Natural History Museum of Los Angeles County, 1993.

Kou, Zhengling. "The Military Line of Genghis Khan (1)," *Beijing Review*, May 16-22, 1994, 26-27.

Krader, Lawrence. "Ecology of Central Asian Pastoralism," *Southwestern Journal of Anthropology*, Vol. 11, No. 4, Winter 1955, pp. 301-326.

Lattimore, Owen. "The Historical Setting of Inner Mongolian Nationalism," *Pacific Affairs*, Vol. 9, Sept. 1936, pp.388-405.

Lattimore, Owen. *Inner Asian Frontiers of China.* London: Oxford University Press, 1940.

Lattimore, Owen. *Introduction to Second Edition of Inner Asian Frontiers of China.* Baltimore: John Hopkins University, 1951, pp. 17-53.

Lattimore, Owen. *Studies in Frontier History: Collected Papers, 1928-1958.* London: Oxford University Press, 1962.

Lattimore, Owen. "The Geography of Chingis Khan," *Geographical Journal*, Vol. CXXIX, Part 1, March 1963, pp.1-7.

Legg, Stuart. *The Heartland.* New York: Farrar, Straus and Giroux, 1971.

Lemonick, Michael D. "Coming Soon: Raiders of the Lost Tomb," *Time*, 26 Sept. 1994, p. 68.

Li, Dun Jen (Ed.). *The Essence of Chinese Civilization.* Toronto: D.Van Nostrand Co.(Canada) Ltd., 1967.

Lin, Ruihan. "The History of Xixia," in *Bianjiang Wenhua Lunji* (A Collection of Papers on the Culture of the Borderland), ed. by Ling, Chunsheng. Taipei: Chinese Culture Publication Committee, 1954, Vol. 2, pp. 295-310 (in Chinese script).

Lister, R.P. *Genghis Khan.* New York: Stein and Day, 1969.

Lo, Hsiang Lin. *Zhongguo Tongshi* (A General History of China). Taipei: Cheng Chung Book Co., 1956 Vol.1 and Vol. 2 (in Chinese script).

Lu, Simian. *Zhongguo Tongshi* (Chinese General History) Vol. 1 and Vol. 2. Hong Kong: Shanghai Book Co., 1976 (in Chinese script).

Ma, Yin. *China's Minority Nationalities.* Beijing: Foreign Languages Press, 1989.

Martin, H. Desmond. *The Rise of Chingis Khan and His Conquest of North China.* New York: Octagon Books, 1971.

Moses, Larry and Stephen A. Halkovic, Jr. *Introduction to Mongolian History and Culture.* Bloomington: Research Institute for Inner Asian Studies, Indiana University, 1985.

Osborn, Henry Fairfield. "The Revival of Central Asiatic Life," *Natural History*, Vol. XXIX, No. 1, 1929, pp. 2-16.

Qian, Mu. *Guoshi Dagan* (A General Chinese History) Vol. 1 and Vol. 2. Taipei: Shangwu Press, 1977 (in Chinese script).

Ren, Mei'e, Yang Renzhang, and Bao Haosheng. *An Outline of China's Physical Geography* (translated by Zhang Tingquan and Hu Genkang). Beijing: Foreign Language Press, 1985.

Ross, Jeffrey A. "The Mongolian People's Republic as a Prototypical Case for the Development of a Comparative Politics of Communist Systems," *The Canada-Mongolia Review*, Vol. IV, No. 1, April 1978, pp. 1-15.

Shakabpa, Tsepon W.D. *Tibet: A Political History.* New Haven: Yale University Press, 1967.

Shi, Jia. "The History of Islam," in *Bianjiang Wenhua Lunji* (A Collection of Papers on the Culture of the Borderland), ed. by Ling, Chunsheng. Taipei: Chinese Culture Publication Committee, 1954, Vol. 3, pp. 416-433 (in Chinese script).

Sinha, Nirmal C. "Historical Status of Tibet," *Bulletin of Tibetology*, Vol. 1, No. 1, 1964, pp. 25-32.

Sinha, Nirmal C. "The Lama," *Bulletin of Tibetology*, Vol. 3, No. 2, 1964, pp. 17-22.

Snellgrove, David L. and H. Richardson. *A Cultural History of Tibet.* London: Weidenfield and Nicholson Ltd., 1968.

Sun, Fukun. *Menggu Jianshi Xinbian* (A New Version of the Brief History of Mongolia). Hong Kong: Freedom Press, 1951 (in Chinese script).

Sun, Jinzhu. *Nei Mongol Dili* (The Geography of Inner Mongolia). Beijing: Kexue Puji Chubanshe, 1957 (in Chinese script).

Tanjun Ranopanza. *The Hidden Tradition: Life Inside the Great Tibetan Monastery Tashihunpo.* Beijing: Foreign Languages Press, 1993.

Waley, A. *Secret History of the Mongols and other Pieces.* London: George Allen and Unwin, 1963.

Walt van Praag, Michael C. *The Status of Tibet.* Boulder: Westview Press, 1987.

Wang, Furen and Suo Wengqing. *Highlights of Tibetan.* Beijing: New World Press, 1984.

Wang, Tsai-tien. "The New Inner Mongolia—Ten Years Old," *People's China*, May 1, 1957, pp. 9-13.

Worden, Robert L. and A.M. Savada (ed.). *Mongolia: A Country Study.* Washington D.C.: Federal Research Division, Library of Congress, 1991.

Wu, En. "Relics of the Northern Nomads, *China Reconstructs*, April 1986, pp. 39-41.

Xie, Bin. *Menggu Wenti* (The Mongolian Questions). Shanghai: Shangwu Press, 1935 (in Chinese script).

Xue Xin. "The Origins of the Mongols and their Descendants," *Zhongguo Bianjiang (China's Borderland)*, Vol. 3, No. 5-6, 1944, pp. 5-8 (in Chinese script).

Yakhontoff, Victor A. "Mongolia: Target or Screen?," *Pacific Affairs*, Vol. 9, March 1936, pp. 13-23.

Yim, S.Y. *Daily Life of a Qing Emperor.* Hong Kong: The Regional Council, 1994.

Zhang, Qiyun. "The Geographical Distribution of Chinese Races," in *Bianjiang Wenhua Lunji* (A Collection of Papers on the Culture of the Borderland), ed. by Ling, Chunsheng. Taipei: Chinese Culture Publication Committee, 1954, Vol. 1, pp. 19-37 (in Chinese script).

Zhang, Xiamin. *Bianjiang Wenti Yu Bianjiang Jianshe* (Border Questions and Border Constructions). Taipei: Chinese Culture Publication Committee, 1957 (in Chinese script).

GLOSSARY

地名、人名、朝代、民族及其他之名稱

(A) DYNASTY	朝代
Zhou	周
Western Zhou	西周
Eastern Zhou	東周
Spring and Autumn period	春秋時代
Warring States period	戰國時代
Qin	秦
Han	漢
Western Han	西漢
Eastern Han	東漢
Three Kingdoms	三國時代
Wei	魏
Shu Han	蜀漢
Wu	吳
Jin	晉
Western Jin	西晉
Eastern Jin	東晉

Han (Former Zhao)	漢〔前趙〕
Northern Liang	北涼
Xia	夏
Former Yan	前燕
Later Yan	後燕
Western Qin	西秦
Southern Liang	南涼
Southern Yan	南燕
Cheng Han	成漢
Former Qin	前秦
Later Liang	後涼
Later Zhao	後趙
Later Qin	後秦
Former Liang	前涼
Western Liang	西涼
Northern Yan	北燕

Northern and Southern Dynasties	南北朝	Later Zhou	後周
Southern dynasties	南朝	Wu	吳
Song	宋	Wu Yue	吳越
Qi	齊	Nan Han	南漢
Liang	梁	Chu	楚
Chen	陳	Qian Shu	前蜀
Northern dynasties	北朝	Min	閩
Northern Wei	北魏	Nan Ping	南平
Eastern Wei	東魏	Hou Shu	後蜀
Western Wei	西魏	Nan Tang	南唐
Northern Qi	北齊	Bei Han	北漢
Northern Zhou	北周	Song	宋
Sui	隋	Northern Song	北宋
Tang	唐	Southern Song	南宋
Five dynasties	五代	Liao	遼
Later Liang	後梁	Jin	金
Later Tang	後唐	Yuan	元
Later Jin	後晉	Ming	明
Later Han	後漢	Qing	清

(B) ETHNIC GROUP AND STATE 民族

Black Qidan (Kara-Khitan)	黑契丹	Kiyat	乞顏部
Dangxiang (Tangut)	黨項	Menggu (Mongol)	蒙古
Daur	達幹爾	Mengwu Shiwei	蒙兀室韋
Di	氐	Merkit	蔑爾乞部
Donghu	東胡	Moge	靺鞨
Ewenti	鄂溫克	Mongol (see Menggu)	蒙古部
Haixi Nuzhen	海西女真	Naiman	乃蠻部
Heishui Moge	黑水靺鞨	Nuzhen	女真
Hui	回	Oirat	瓦剌
Huiqi	回訖	Onggut	汪古部
Huigu	回鶻	Pohai	渤海國
Jianzhou Nuzhen	建州女真	Qiang	羌
Jie	羯	Qidan (Khitan)	契丹
Kara-Khitan (see Black Qidan)	黑契丹	Quan Rong	犬戎
Kereit	克烈	Ruanruan	蠕蠕
Khalkha	喀爾喀	Sheng Nuzhen	生女真
Khitan (see Qidan)	契丹	Shiwei	室韋
Kirghiz	柯爾克孜	Shu Nuzhen	熟女真
		Sumo Moge	粟末靺鞨

Tabgach Xianbei	拓跋鮮卑	**(C) PERSON**	人名
Tangut (see Dangxiang)	黨項	Aisin Gioro	愛新覺羅
Tantan (see Tatar)	塔塔爾部(韃靼)	Altan Khan	俺答可汗
Tatar (Tantan)	韃靼	Esen Khan	也先可汗
Tufan (Tibetan)	吐蕃(西藏)	Genghis Khan	成吉思汗
Tujue	突厥	Han Wendi	漢文帝
Tuoba Xianbei	拓跋鮮卑	Han Wudi	漢武帝
Tuyuhun	吐谷渾	Han Yuandi	漢元帝
Uygurs	維吾爾(畏吾兒)	Huangtaiji	皇太極
Wuhuan	烏恆	Huhanye Chanyu	呼韓邪單于
Xianbei	鮮卑	Jin Gongdi	晉恭帝
Xiliao	西遼國	Jin Yuandi	晉元帝
Xiongnu	匈奴	Jincheng	金城公主
Xiqiang	西羌	Li Jing	李靖
Xixia	西夏國	Liu Yao	劉曜
Yeren Nuzhen	野人女真	Liu Yu	劉裕
Yuezhi	月氏	Liu Yuan	劉淵
Zhuang	壯	Maodun	冒頓
		Mengtian	蒙恬

Ming Muzong	明穆宗	Tuoba Gui	拓跋珪
Ogodai	窩闊台	Ulanfu	烏蘭夫
Qin Shi Huang	秦始皇	Wang Zhaojun	王昭君
Shaboluo Khan	沙鉢羅可汗	Wanyan Aguda	完顏阿骨打
Shi Jingtang	石敬塘	Wencheng	文成公主
Shunyi Wang	順義王	Xieli Khan	頡利可汗
Shunzhi	順治	Yelu Dashi	耶律大石
Sonam Gyatso	索南嘉措	Yesugei Khaldun	也速該
Song Gaozong	宋高宗	Yong Le	永樂
Song Gongdi	宋恭帝	Yuan Shik-k'ai	袁世凱
Song Huizong	宋徽宗	Yuan Shizu	元世祖
Song Qinzong	宋欽宗	Yuan Taizu	元太祖
Song Zhenzong	宋真宗	Zhao Gou	趙構
Songtsen Gampo	松贊干布	Zhou Pingwang	周平王
Sun Yat-sen	孫逸仙	Zhu Yuanzhang	朱元璋
Tang Gaozong	唐高宗	Zhu Wen	朱溫
Tang Taizong	唐太宗		
Temujin	鐵木真		
Tride Tsutsen	棄隸縮贊		

(D) PLACE NAMES AND OTHER NAMES　地名、及其他之名稱

Alashan Meng	阿拉善盟	Hetao Man	河套人
Balinzuo Banner	巴林左旗	Hetian	和田
Baotou	包頭市	Hexi Corridor	河西走廊
Bayannaoer Meng	巴彥淖爾盟	Hohhot	呼和浩特市
Beijing	北京	Hongshan Culture	紅山文化
Burkhan Khaldun	不兒罕合勒敦山(汗山)	Houtao	後套
Chanyu	單于	Hulunbeier Meng	呼倫貝爾盟
Chifeng	赤峰市	Jiankang	建康
Dadu	大都	Jokhang Monastery	大昭寺
Datong	大同	Karakorum	哈拉和林
Dongsheng	東勝	Kerulen River	克魯倫河
Ejin Horo Qi	伊金霍洛旗	Khan	可汗
Gelugpa	黃教(格魯派)	Kueisui (see Hohhot)	歸綏市
Guangxi	廣西	Kulun (see Urga)	庫倫
Hangzhou	杭州	Laoha River	老哈河
Haojing	鎬京	Liaoyang	遼陽
Helin (see Karakorum)	和林	Lin'an	臨安
		Liujiang Man	柳江人
		Luoyang	洛陽

75

Luoyi	洛邑	Wulanchabu Meng	烏蘭察布盟
Nanjing	南京	Xiajiadian	夏家店
Ningcheng	寧城	Xilamulun River	西拉木倫河
Ningxia	寧夏	Xilinguole Meng	錫林郭勒盟
Onon River	鄂嫩河	Xing Zhong Hui	興中會
Ordos Man (see Hetao Man)	河套人	Xingan Meng	興安盟
Pagor Street	八角街	Xinjiang Uygur Autonomous Region	新疆
Pingcheng	平城	Yangshao Culture	仰韶文化
Qilinshan Man	祁連山人	Yangzhou	揚州
Qinghai	青海	Yanjing	燕京
Sakyapa	花教(薩迦派)	Yanyun Shiliuzhou	燕雲十六州
Shangdu	上都	Yikezhao Meng	伊克昭盟
Shengjing	盛京	Yinchuan	銀川
Shenyang	瀋陽	Yumen	玉門
Ulaan Baatar (Ulan Bator)	烏蘭巴托	Zhelinmu Meng	哲里木盟
Ulanhad (see Chifeng)	烏蘭哈	Zhenglan Banner	正藍旗
Urga	阿加市	Zhongdu	中都
Wuhai	烏海市		
Wuhu Luanhua	五胡亂華		

THE AUTHOR

David Chuenyan Lai was born in Guangzhou, China. After he finished his matriculation at King's College, Hong Kong, he was awarded a Hong Kong Government Scholarship to attend the University of Hong Kong, where he received his B.A. (1st Class Honours) in Geography and Geology in 1960, and M.A. in Industrial Geography four years later. Then, through a British Commonwealth Scholarship, he attended the London School of Economics and Political Science, University of London in 1964. He received his Ph.D. in 1967, specializing in Urban Geography and the Regional Geography of China. Dr. Lai taught at the University of Hong Kong for one year before he and his wife, Roberta Manyuk, emigrated to Canada and became Canadian citizens in 1973. He joined the University of Victoria in 1968, and attained the rank of Professor in 1989. Dr. Lai has taught summer schools also at the University of Hawaii, the University of Alberta, Lakehead University, Memorial University of Newfoundland, and the University of Toronto. He has visited China more than ten times and led a group of teachers and students on a tour around the country in the summer of 1984.

Dr. Lai's research and publishing interests are Chinatowns, Overseas Chinese, Hong Kong and China. Of his more than 140 publications, nearly half relate to Chinatowns and Chinese communities in Canada. His books include *Chinatowns: Towns Within Cities in Canada*, published by the University of British Columbia Press in 1988; *Arches in British Columbia*, published by Sono Nis Press, 1982; and *The Forbidden City Within Victoria—Myth, Symbol and Streetscape of Canada's Earliest Chinatown*, published by Orca Book Publishers, 1991.

Dr. Lai has been a consultant to Edmonton's Planning Department on the Chinatown Gateway Project; Portland's Development Commission on Chinatown Redevelopment Project; Kamloops' Department of Parks on the preservation and beautification of the Chinese Cemetery, Ottawa's Planning Department on the proposed new Chinatown on Somerset Street West; and the Royal British Museum on the Chinatown Exhibit. He carried out the translations of the Chinese manuscripts about Chee Kung Tong for Barkerville Historic Town, and the preliminary study of the Yip Sang Collections for the Vancouver City Archives.

Dr. Lai is very active in community work, serving as a director of the Chinese Public School (1977-1993), Chair of the Chinatown Redevelopment Committee (1980-1993), a member of the Heritage Advisory Committee of City of Victoria (1979-1988), Chair of Saanich's Heritage Advisory and Archival Committee (1983 and 1989), Vice-Chair of Victoria's Sister City Advisory and Liaison Committee (1989 and 1990), and Chair of Victoria's Twinned City Advisory Committee (1993). He has been the academic advisor of the Chinese Consolidated Benevolent Association of Victoria since 1977. In 1989 Dr. Lai was appointed as an Honorary Overseas Advisor of the Society of Overseas Chinese Studies, Guangdong Province, China. He is currently the National Director of the National Congress of Chinese Canadians in Canada and the Director of the Chinese Benevolent Association of Canada (National Headquarters).

Dr. Lai was named an Honourary Citizen by the City of Victoria in 1980, and conferred C.M. (Member of Order of Canada) by Governor-General Edward Schreyer in 1983. In addition, he has received many other awards in recognition of his Chinatown research and community work. For example, he was awarded an Applied Geography Citation Award by the Association of American Geographers in 1982. In the same year he received a Regional Community Service Award from the Heritage Canada Foundation. In 1983, he was given an Award of Merit by the American Association of State and Local History, and many certifications of merits or other awards from the Victoria Chinatown Lions Club, Hallmark Society, Greater Victoria Chamber of Commerce, Chinese Consolidated Benevolent Association of Victoria, Chinese Benevolent Association of Vancouver, etc. for his contributions to the community. In 1984, Dr. Lai received a Certificate of Merit from the British Columbia Historical Federation for "historical writing." In 1992, he received the Commemorative Medal for the 125th Anniversary of Canadian Federation from Governor-General Ramon John Hnatyshyn given for professional achievement and significant contributions to the community and society.

塞外民族之興衰

黎全恩